KW-242-111

Tran thi Ai Cam

International Tourism and Management

Tran thi Ai Cam

International Tourism and Management

Explaining tourists satisfaction and intention to revisit Nha Trang, Viet Nam

LAP LAMBERT Academic Publishing

Impressum/Imprint (nur für Deutschland/only for Germany)
Bibliografische Information der Deutschen Nationalbibliothek: Die Deutsche
Nationalbibliothek verzeichnet diese Publikation in der Deutschen Nationalbibliografie;
detaillierte bibliografische Daten sind im Internet über http://dnb.d-nb.de abrufbar.
Alle in diesem Buch genannten Marken und Produktnamen unterliegen warenzeichen-,
marken- oder patentrechtlichem Schutz bzw. sind Warenzeichen oder eingetragene
Warenzeichen der jeweiligen Inhaber. Die Wiedergabe von Marken, Produktnamen,
Gebrauchsnamen, Handelsnamen, Warenbezeichnungen u.s.w. in diesem Werk berechtigt
auch ohne besondere Kennzeichnung nicht zu der Annahme, dass solche Namen im Sinne
der Warenzeichen- und Markenschutzgesetzgebung als frei zu betrachten wären und
daher von jedermann benutzt werden dürften.

Coverbild: www.ingimage.com

Verlag: LAP LAMBERT Academic Publishing GmbH & Co. KG
Heinrich-Böcking-Str. 6-8, 66121 Saarbrücken, Deutschland
Telefon +49 681 3720-310, Telefax +49 681 3720-3109
Email: info@lap-publishing.com

Approved by: Ai Cam, University of Nha Trang, 2011

Herstellung in Deutschland (siehe letzte Seite)
ISBN: 978-3-659-10784-9

Imprint (only for USA, GB)
Bibliographic information published by the Deutsche Nationalbibliothek: The Deutsche
Nationalbibliothek lists this publication in the Deutsche Nationalbibliografie; detailed
bibliographic data are available in the Internet at http://dnb.d-nb.de.
Any brand names and product names mentioned in this book are subject to trademark,
brand or patent protection and are trademarks or registered trademarks of their respective
holders. The use of brand names, product names, common names, trade names, product
descriptions etc. even without a particular marking in this works is in no way to be
construed to mean that such names may be regarded as unrestricted in respect of
trademark and brand protection legislation and could thus be used by anyone.

Cover image: www.ingimage.com

Publisher: LAP LAMBERT Academic Publishing GmbH & Co. KG
Heinrich-Böcking-Str. 6-8, 66121 Saarbrücken, Germany
Phone +49 681 3720-310, Fax +49 681 3720-3109
Email: info@lap-publishing.com

Printed in the U.S.A.
Printed in the U.K. by (see last page)
ISBN: 978-3-659-10784-9

EXPLAINING TOURISTS SATISFACTION AND INTENTION TO REVISIT NHA TRANG, VIET NAM

TRAN THI AI CAM

Master Thesis in Fisheries and Aquaculture

Management and Economics

(30 ECTS)

The Norwegian College of Fishery Science

University of Tromso, Norway

&

Nha Trang University, Vietnam

May 2011

ACKNOWLEDGEMENTS

I would like to thank the many people who helped me accomplish this thesis. First, and foremost, I want Professor Svein Ottar Olsen, University of Tromso to know how much I appreciate his faithful guidance and unsurpassed expertise from the beginning to the end of the thesis writing. I especially would like to express my gratitude to him for his full enthusiastic supervisor. I could not have finished my thesis without his guidance and assistance.

I also would like to thank Dr. Ho Huy Tuu, my external supervisor, Nha Trang University. Who commended and helped me in the data analyzing process.

During the two years study programme at Nha Trang University, I am grateful to the financial supports of Norwegian government, the scholarship via the Norad Project.

In additionally, I would also like to thank my friend, Huynh Thi Ngoc Diep, who has assisted and encouraged me during the thesis writing period.

There are also a lot of people that I would like to thanks. They are my teachers, my mother and my colleagues. Especially, my mother, who has given me unconditional love and support throughout my life.

Nha Trang, May, 2011

Best regards,

Tran Thi Ai Cam

TABLE OF CONTENTS

LIST OF TABLES

LIST OF FIGURES

ABSTRACT

The first purpose of the thesis is to find how visitors evaluate the quality of different facets or attributes of a destination image of Nha Trang, how satisfied they are with Nha Trang, loyalty intention to revisit and willingness to recommend Nha Trang to others. The second is to investigate what "image" is most important to explain global satisfaction with visiting Nha Trang. The third is to investigate how perceived quality, satisfaction and other motivational or dismotivational factors (e.g., demographic characteristics, variety seeking) influence loyalty intention to revisit and willingness to recommend to others.

The measurement scales used here were adapted from previous studies found in the literature. The survey was conducted in Nha Trang, Vietnam, with sample of 201 respondents. The study has used the EFA, CFA supported by the Amos 16.0 software to test the reliability, convergent and discriminate validity and SEM to test the relationships.

This study found that local food, environment and culture & social factors are attractive to tourists while tourist leisure & entertainment and infrastructure & accessibilty factors are not attractive to them. Tourists may have not strong satisfaction with visiting Nha Trang. Tourists felt satisfied with visiting Nha Trang, they have intented to recommed higher than to revisit. The findings indicated that environment factor carried the heaviest weight for tourists satisfaction. Structural equation modeling identified that environment, local food and culture & social are significantly related to positive satisfaction. While tourist leisure & entertainment and infrastructure & accessibilty has non significant, positive impact to satisfaction. Moreover, the study found that perceived quality and variety seeking are significant and positive related to satisfaction, age had a negative influence on satisfaction and intention to revisit, and satisfaction is significant and positive related to intention to revisit and recommendation.

The study provides useful information for local authorities and tourism marketers in Nha Trang. From here, some strategies for promoting and improving international visitors satisfaction and intentional loyalty.

Keywords: destination image, tourists satisfaction, intentional loyalty, Nha Trang.

Chapter 1

INTRODUCTION

1.1 Managerial background

Tourism is identified as one of the most potential industries of Vietnamese economy (Source: *http://www.cinet.vn/upLoadFile/HTML/main.htm*). Tourism is considered to be a top priority for the following reasons. Firstly, it is the industry requiring more labor, thus it provides more jobs for city residents, by which it helps to solve unemployment for society. Secondly, it is the industry bringing to many important benefits, improving social-economic situation, enhancing income for people. Thirdly, it can promote peace, enhancing understanding together and building a unified and sustainable   country.   And   so   on   (Source: *http://www.cinet.vn/upLoadFile/HTML/main.htm*).

Although Vietnam's tourism industry is still young in compared with the one of other Southeast Asia countries, it has made progressed and contributed significantly to economic development and social progress of the nation. In the context of international integration, the Vietnam government has focused on developing for tourism industry, enhancing   service   quality,   expanding   operations   scale.   (Source: *http://thuvienluanvan.com*, thesis code TH2509).

The numbers of tourists to Vietnam have increased significantly from 2000 to 2010. Specifically, there were about 2,140,100 tourists in 2000, which increased to 3,467,757 by 2005 (Vietnam National Administration of tourism, 2007). The Vietnamese national Administration of Tourism 2010 reported that the number of international visitors to Vietnam of the year 2010 was about 5,049,855 people, which increased 34.8% compared to 2009. Among them, the majority were from the China (rise 74.5%), Thai Lan (rise 39.7%), Korea (rise 37.7%), Japan (rise 24%), Taiwan (rise 23.7%) and the rest came from America, Australia, Cambodia, Malaysia, France and other countries around the world   (Source: General Statistics Office Vietnamese tourism, 2010). According to the Department of Culture – Sports and Tourism Khanh Hoa (posted on the website of the tourism promotion center in Khanh Hoa), the growth rate of international tourists visited Nha Trang – Khanh Hoa in 2010 only reached 11.13%

compared to 2009. This was a very low figure if compared to the average growth of the country. Why?

The global tourism industry has evolved into an area of fierce competition, and a fundamental challenge for marketers is to comprehend the distinguishing characteristics of tourist experiences (Perdue, 2002). Towards the tourism industry of Vietnam, to survive in fierce international environment and compete with the tourism development in the region and the world, the authoriries and Gorvernment need to do many things. Firstly, they have been establishing the strength based on improving sustainable competitive advantages national. Secondly, they have been seeking many solution overcome disadvantages of industry (*http://thuvienluanvan.com*, thesis code TH2509) and trying to keep up with the development speed of nations which has more progressive in tourism.

Therefore, what motivate do tourists visit/revisit Nhatrang – Vietnam? This can be done in several ways. For example. In order to meet the competition from other tourist destinations around the world, the tourism industry in Nha Trang needs to understand tourists preferences and motives for choosing Nha Trang as their visit alternative. What are their main motivation for visiting Nha Trang and how do they evaluate Nha Trang as a tourist destination? For the tourism industry, it is also important to know if they intend to return or revisit Nha Trang and if they recommend this destination to others.

1.2 Theoretical background

Destination image, perceived quality, perceived value and satisfaction (Bigne et al., 2001; Pike, 2002; Chen & Tsai, 2007; Chi & Qu, 2008; Chen & Chen, 2010) are the most frequent factors used to explain tourist motivation or intention to visit/revisit a tourist destination. Customer satisfaction is one of the most frequently examined topics in the hospitality and tourism field because it plays an important role in survival and future of any tourism products and services (Gursoy, McCleary & Lepsito, 2003). It also significantly influences the choice of destination, the consumption of products and services, and the decision to return (Kozak & Rimmington, 2000).

Those perceptions, evaluations or experiences are in the literature defined differently such as destination image (Baloglu & McCleary, 1999; Chen & Tsai, 2007; Bigne et al., 2009; Wnag & Hsu, 2010), perceived quality (Bigne et al., 2009; Quintal &

Polczynski, 2011; Valazques et al., 2011), perceived value (Gallarza & Saura, 2006; Chen & Tsai, 2007; Bigne et al., 2009; Chen & Chen, 2010), attribute satisfaction (Gallarza & Saura, 2006; Chen & Tsai, 2007; Bigne et al., 2009; Chen & Chen, 2010; Wnag & Hsu, 2010; Quintal & Polczynski, 2011; Valazques et al., 2011), or behavioral intentions (Chen & Tsai, 2007; Bigne et al., 2009; Wnag & Hsu, 2010; Chen & Chen, 2010) depending on the theoretical and empirical focus of the studies.

Those variables are in some studies used as independent or integrated predictors of intention to visit or revisit, willingness to pay/ willingness to recommend (Valle et al., 2006) or positive word of mouth communication (Boulding et al., 1993; Zeithaml, Berry & Parasurama, 1996), loyalty (Gallarza & Saura, 2006; Valazques et al., 2011). Foe example, studies of international visitors (Chinese) in Vietnam have focused on factors such as perception, satisfaction and destination loyalty (behavioural intention) (Truong & King, 2009).

Other factors or variables are identified as drivers of motivators of consumers intention to visit a general (e.g., country) or specific destination (e.g., a city, natural of rural) as well as an event (e.g., sea festival, miss earth). Those factors are for example personal characteristics (Baloglu & McCleary, 1999; Beerli & Martin, 2004), perceived risk (Quintal & Polczynski, 2011), variety seeking (Bigne et al., 2008), personal values (Pitts & Woodside, 1986; Ekinci & Chen, 2002). In this study, the author will focus mainly on the measurement of attributes destination, variety seeking factors and demographic characteristics affect to tourist satisfaction and intentional loyalty. Variety seeking plays a key role in the comprehension of tourist behavior, affecting satisfaction and their intention to return to the same destination in the future (Niininen et al., 2004). The relationship between variety seeking and satisfaction and loyalty in services is an under-researched topic in the marketing literature (Berne´ et al., 2001, 2005). Many researchers conceive variety seeking as an individual trait (Berne´ et al., 2001, 2005; Kahn, 1995). Tourists with a high variety seeking propensity will show a varied pattern of destination choice. (Bigne et al., 2009).

Nha Trang is identified as one of the 10 tourism centers of the whole country (Source: service of culture, sport and tourism Khanh Hoa). It advantages are based on unique characteristics and potential such as beautiful scenery, fresh air, fresh food, so on. In recent years, the Khanh Hoa province has organized many cultural and tourism events, such as the sea festivals, the beauty competition (examples, Miss Earth 2010 at

Vinpearl land), etc. With these advantages, local authorities thought that the numbers of international tourists come to Nha Trang – Khanh Hoa rise highly, but the reality is not. Why does the growth rate of international tourists to Nha Trang – Khanh Hoa increase slowly? How to accelerate the growth of tourists? In order to answers such questions, the tourism industry and Government need to learn how tourists evaluate different facilities in Nha Trang, what is the most important drivers for visiting Nha Trang, and do this drivers vary between different segments of visitors. For example, Truong & Foster (2006) analyzed tourist satisfaction by focusing on factors such as culture, political, tourist infrastructure and atmosphere.

1.3 Purposes of the study

The purposes of this study are threefold. The first is to find how visitors evaluate the quality of different facets or attributes of a destination image of Nha Trang, how satisfied they are with Nha Trang, loyalty intention to revisit and willingness to recommend Nha Trang to others (friends and relative). This will be done in a descriptive format. The second is to investigate what "image" is most important to explain global satisfaction with visiting Nha Trang The third will investigate how perceived quality, satisfaction and other motivational or dismotivational factors (e.g., demographic characteristics and variety seeking) influence loyalty intention to revisit and willingness to recommend to others. Finally, this study will discuss implication and strategies for promoting and improving visitors satisfaction and intentional loyalty of previous and potential tourists visiting Nha Trang.

During recent years, Khanh Hoa province has done mostly national promotion of Nha Trang as a tourist destination. However, more and more international tourists are visiting Nha Trang and knowledge about their motivations to visit this city is not previously investigated (Source: *http://www.nhatrang-travel.com/index*). Except, Kim Lien (2010) considered that motivations of tourists visited to Nha Trang in order to satisfied their needs of enjoying a good time with others, building friendships, and discovering new places and increasing knowledge. Hence, this study will only survey international tourists.

1.4 Method

Subject and scope of research: international tourists who have been visiting and revisit to Nha Trang city, a famous tourism destination in Vietnam, in March and April, in 2011. And tourists are 18 years old and over.

The survey questionnaire consists of five sections, including all factors in model of study, was designed to explain tourists satisfaction and intention to visit/ revisit or recommendation the journey to others. Sample size of surveys was at 250. Some questionnaires were delivered to some hotels where foreign tourists take a rest. And some rest questionnaires were interviewed directly tourists at some famous restaurants, coffee & bar and Nha Trang beach.

Items to measure the constructs were adopted from the previous studies and revised to appropriate to characteristic of Nha Trang. In analyzing the data, first presented travel and demographic characteristic. Second, descriptive analysis to evaluate Nha Trang as a destination. Then analyzing EFA, CFA, to test reliability, convergent validity and discriminate validity. Finally, the relationships were tested by structural equation modeling (SEM). The data were analyzed by SPSS 16.0 and Amos 16.0.

1.5 Structure of thesis

This thesis will be divided into five parts. The first part is the introduction chapter, the managerial background, theorical background, purposes of the thesis, method and structure of thesis will briefly be introduced. In the second part is conceptual framework chapter, will represent the concepts of some variable in intentional loyalty, tourists satisfaction, destination image & perceived quality of destination attributes, facets of tourist destination, variety seeking and tourists satisfaction, demographic characteristics and tourists satisfaction/ loyalty and concept model. In the third part is methodology chapter, this chapter will be described the methods used to investigste, data collecting procedure, the measurement and techniques for the main concepts. The fourth part is the results chapter, the results from empirical survey will be explained and the last part is the discussion and conclusion of this thesis.

Chapter 2

CONCEPTUAL FRAMEWORK

This study concentrates on identifying the destination attributes, variety seeking and personal characteristics which influence satisfaction and intentional loyalty of tourists toward intention to revisit or recommend destination to others.

There are many different definitions of and theoretical approaches to studying destination image formation. For example, Lawson and Baud – Bovy, (1977) defined a destination image as the expression of all knowledge, impressions, prejudices and emotional thoughts an individual or group has of a particular object or place. Whereas Embacher & Buttle, (1989) defined image is comprised of the ideas or conceptions held individually or collectively of the destination under investigation. Image may comprise both cognitive and evaluative components. Moreover, Um & Crompton, (1990) describe destination image as a gestalt or holistic construct. Reilly, (1990) emphasises the total impression a place makes on the minds of others. Following Rispoli & Tamma, 1991, 1995 quoted in Franch, 2002 express that destination image is as a global construct; it is presented as an aggregate of resources, structures, activities joined with each other. This is the meaning of global product, which is a specific and spatially-defined set, containing all the attractive factors (goods, services, information, natural and social resources) (Parroco et al., 2005). In this study, the author define destination image as perceived quality evaluation of a combination of five different attributes/facets such as environment, infrastructure & accessibility, culture & social, tourist leisure & entertainment and local food.

Satisfaction has always been considered essential for business success. However, interest in studying the measurement of satisfaction has moved towards the concept of loyalty, as it enables better prediction of consumer behaviour which is key to business continuity (Chi & Qu, 2008). Past studies have suggested that perceptions of service quality and value affect satisfaction, and satisfaction furthermore affect loyalty and post-behaviors (Oliver, 1980; Cronin & Taylor, 1992; Fornell, 1992; Anderson & Sullivan, 1993; Tam, 2000; Bignie, Sanchez & Sanchez, 2001; Petrick & Backman, 2002; Chen & Tsai, 2007; Chen, 2008; De Rojas & Camarero, 2008). For example, the satisfied tourists may revisit a destination, recommend it to others. On the other hand, dissatisfied tourists may not return to the same destination and may not recommend it to other tourists (Reisinger & Turner, 2003).

Some studies show that the revisit intention is explained by the number of previous visits (Mazurki, 1989; Court & Lupton, 1997; Petrick et al., 2001). Oh, (1999) establishes service quality, perceived price, customer value and perceptions of company performance as determinants of customer satisfaction is used to explain revisit intentions. Um et al., (2006) propose a structural equation model that explains revisiting intentions as determined by satisfaction, perceived attractiveness, perceived quality of service and perceived value for money. This study will be applied structural equation model that explaining destination image and tourists satisfaction toward intention to revisit or recommendatin Nha Trang to others.

Based on the previous research, the study propose as the most general model is shown in figure 2.1

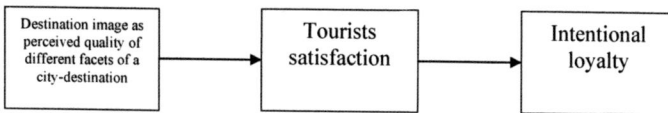

Figure 2.1: The quality – satisfaction – loyalty model (adapted from Chi & Qu, 2008; Wnag & Hsu, 2010; Valle et al., 2006)

Recent research suggests that the relationship between satisfaction and intentional loyalty may have several moderators or mediators (e.g., Homburg & Giering, 2001). In addition factors above, in the consumer behaviour literature, consumers' need for variety has been a relevant issue (Chen & Paliwoda, 2004). This can have a big impact on consumer behaviour and its influence on satisfaction and loyalty (Riley et al., 2001). Oliver, (1999) suggests that loyalty can be studied as a chain from cognitive loyalty (e.g. price and quality), affective loyalty (general evaluation or attitude), conative loyalty (a desire to intend an action) and action loyalty. This study will include that three first phases of this hierarchical model.

In the following, the author will discuss the constructs and relationships more in detail and with a special focus on literature from tourist marketing.

2.1 Intentional loyalty

Loyalty has been defined and measured in many different ways (Jacoby & Chestnut, 1978). Loyalty is conceptualized from three main perspectives: behavioural, attitudinal and compound (Bowen & Chen, 2001; Zins, 2001). Behavioural loyalty is reflected in repeat purchase, attitudinal loyalty includes recommending the service provider to others and repurchase intentions, and compound loyalty combines both components, predicting the construct better (Dimitriades, 2006; Pritchard & Howard, 1997).

According to Oliver's definition (1997), loyalty is understood from the behavioural point of view as it refers to the future product or service repeat purchase commitment despite situational influences and marketing efforts directed at causing changes in behaviour (p.392). To Berne´, (1997), loyalty is a promise of the individual referred to his behaviour which entails future purchase likelihood or less likelihood of changing to another brand or service provider. As mentioned above, Oliver, (1999) divided loyalty to four phases: cognitive loyalty, affective loyalty, conative loyalty and action loyalty. In practice, conative loyalty is defined as the customers' behavioral intention to keep on using the brand in the future (Pedersen & Nysveen, 2001). Because many national and international tourist one visit Nha Trang once or very seldom, this study defines loyalty as intentional (Guenzi & Pelloni, 2004) – as intention to revisit.

Satisfied customers are more likely to recommend friends, relatives or other potential customers to a product/service by acting as free word of mouth advertising agents (Shoemaker & Lewis, 1999). The degree of destination loyalty is frequently reflected in tourists' intentions to revisit the destination and in their willingness to recommend it (Chen & Tsai, 2007; Oppermann, 2000). The benefits of loyalty have traditionally been highlighted in the literature from a temporary perspective, as they have significant present and future value for company profits and continuity (Valazques et al., 2011). In the short term, loyal customers spend more with the service provider (O'Brien & Jones, 1995) and in the long term, they attract new customers by word of mouth (Reichheld & Teal, 1996). This study will also define intention to revisit and recommend Nha Trang to others as a facet of the intentional loyalty construct.

2.2 Tourist satisfaction

It is important to make clear the meaning of tourist satisfaction in this study. There are many definitions of satisfaction, it is generally recognised as a post-purchase construct that is related to how much a consumer likes or dislikes a service or product after experiencing it (Woodside, Frey & Daly, 1989). Weber, (1996) has proposed consumer satisfaction as a fundamental pillar of marketing theory and as a key influence over future purchase intentions, market share and word of mouth (WOM) communication. Parasuraman, Zeithaml & Berry, (1994) claim that a customer's overall satisfaction may be related to their assessment of not only service quality (e.g. courtesy, responsiveness, etc.) but also product features (e.g. size of hotel room, etc.) and price. On the other hand, many researchers distinguish conceptualizations of customer satisfaction between transaction-specific and their global or cumulative evaluation of the service (e.g., Holbrook & Corfman, 1985; Boulding et al., 1993). To transaction-specific perspective, customer satisfaction is a post-choice evaluative judgment of a specific purchase occasion (Oliver, 1980, 1993). By comparison, cumulative customer satisfaction is an overall evaluation based on the total purchase and consumption experience with a good or service over time (Fornell, 1992; Bitner & Hubbert, 1994). Thus, satisfaction is a multifaceted concept (Truong & Foster, 2006, Truong & King, 2009).

In content of tourism, satisfaction has been found to be the outcome of the comparison between expectations and experiences (Truong & Foster, 2006). Satisfaction is primarily referred to as a function of pre-travel expectations and post-travel experiences (Pizam, Neumann & Reichel, 1978). When experiences compared to expectations result in feelings of gratification, the tourist is satisfied (Reisinger & Turner, 2003) and leave that destination with their good memory. Even, they agree to pay more for this service. However, when they result in feelings of displeasure, the tourist is dissatisfied (Reisinger & Turner, 2003). This is a reason to explain why tourism industry are determined to highlight a destination in order to enhance the satisfaction of visitors. For example, Chon, (1989) examined tourist satisfaction by comparing travelers' previous images of the destination and what they actually see, feel and achieve at the destination. He reported that tourist satisfaction is the result of the relationship between tourists' expectations about the destination based on their previous images of the destination and their evaluation of the outcome of their experience at the destination area. Most study define and measure the experience part of satisfaction only. This will also be done in this study. The author intend to include expectation as one item of a global satisfaction construct.

Pizam, Neumann & Reichel, (1978) stated that it is important to measure consumer satisfaction with each attraction of the destination, because consumer satisfaction or not with one of the attraction leads to satisfaction or not with the destination. Because the model in this study define destination image as the evaluation (quality performance) of each attraction or attributes with an attraction. The author will not intent to define satisfaction as an attribute evaluation as some studies prefer (e.g., Chen & Chen, 2010; Wnag & Hsu, 2010). In my theoretical approach, it is much the same as destination image the way the author intent to define and measure it.

2.3 Tourist satisfaction – intentional loyalty relationships

Most studies confirm that satisfaction with a tourist experience contributes positively to loyalty (Pritchard & Howard, 1997; Oppermann, 2000; Alexandris et al., 2006; Yuksel, 2007; Chi & Qu, 2008). The relationship between satisfaction and loyalty also depends on how satisfaction and loyalty are measured. For example, a few empirical studies that have tested the relationship between satisfaction and perceived or actual behavioural loyalty (not attitudinal) have found a moderate to low relationship (e.g., Mittal & Kamakura, 2001). Although satisfaction does not guarantee loyalty, it is true that loyal customers are satisfied (Jones & Sasser, 1995).

Satisfaction and loyalty can be measured by revisited or by recommendation to other consumers (friends and family who are potential tourists) (Pine et. al., 1995; Yoon & Uysal, 2005). Empirical research reports that tourist satisfaction is a good indicator of intentions to revisit and recommend to others (Kozak & Rimmington, 2000; Yoon & Uysal, 2005; San Martin et al., 2008). Other studies find significant effects of satisfaction on the willingness to pay more and the intensity of the service experience (Bigne' et al., 2008) and a very strong relationship with positive word of mouth (Macintosh, 2007). This is a reason to explain why satisfaction and loyalty have been seen as one of the more important indicators of companies success. Because satisfaction and loyalty are key to long term survival (Nicholls et al., 1998) and future of any tourism products and services (Gursoy et al., 2003, 2007). It can help managers to improve services (Fornell, 1992). In addition, the ability of managing feedback received from customers can be an important source of competitive advantage (Peters, 1994).

Recently, more holistic models have been used to explain destination loyalty in tourism research. For example, Yoon & Uysal, (2005) propose a model which relates destination loyalty with travel satisfaction and holiday motivations. Their study finds a significant cause-effect relationship between travel satisfaction and destination loyalty as well as between motivations and travel satisfaction. The degree of destination loyalty is frequently reflected in tourists' intentions to revisit the destination (Oppermann, 2000; Chen & Tsai, 2007). Loyalty is the result of satisfaction and this is shown by several studies in the area of services (Mattila, 2001).

2.4 Destination image as perceived quality of destination attributes

The image concept has generally been considered as an attitudinal construct consisting of an individual's mental representation of knowledge (beliefs), feelings, and global impression about an object or destination (Baloglu & McCleary, 1999). Researchers in several disciplines and fields agree that the image construct has both perceptual/cognitive and affective evaluations. The perceptual/cognitive evaluations refer to the beliefs or knowledge about a destination's attributes, whereas the affective image represents a tourist's feelings toward a destination (Russell, 1980; Walmsley & Jenkins, 1993; Baloglu & Brinberg, 1997; Baloglu & McCleary, 1999b). Gartner, (1993) proposes that the affective component usually becomes operational during the evaluation stage of the destination selection process. In the context of tourism, Baloglu and McCleary, (1999a, b) and Stern & Krakover, (1993) show empirically that the affective evaluations have a direct influence on the overall image. However, in this study, the author focuses primarily on perceptual/cognitive evaluations to image.

By other approaches, based on this conceptual framework, destination image is defined as not only the perceptions of individual destination attributes but also the holistic impression made by the destination (Echtner & Ritchie, 2003). Destination image consists of functional characteristics (such as: scenery, attractions, accommodation facilities, price levels), concerning psychological characteristics and the more tangible aspects of the destination (such as: level of friendliness, quality of service expected, fame, etc), or concerning the more intangible aspects (such as: friendliness, safety, atmosphere). On the other hand, images of destinations can include unique features and events (Echtner & Ritchie, 2003). This conceptualisation of destination images applied to the Nha Trang – Vietnam as an example. The image of Nha Trang city consideres as a event and travel destination. Nha Trang' image include various functional and psychological characteristics such as many kind of luxury accommadation (Sunrise hotel, Sheraton, etc), beautiful beach, fresh and delicious food (special is fresh seafood), warm climate, safety, friendliness of people, etc. In this study, the author want to define destination image as a combination of attributes of tourist destination – as perceived quality of different attributes with a destination. The global definition is included in a satisfaction construct.

Moreover, according to Day & Crash, (2000); Oh, (2003) considered that perceived quality and perceived value are these variables which best explains satisfaction and loyalty. We can define variables to the following. First variable is perceived quality. According to Oliver, (1997), the perceived quality is influenced by the expectations of the consumer. While expectations can be seen as beliefs that the consumer use to make about results or performance of the product in the future (Olson & Dover, 1979). Parasuraman et al., (1985) defined perceived quality as an attitude that results from the comparison of consumer expectations with the actual performance. To tourism research, the perceived quality of a holiday destination has been viewed as a combination of tourists' trip experiences and perceived service received in relation to their expectations of the actual service performance (Bolton & Drew, 1991). Thus, perceived quality can be considered as the outcome of the evaluation process of the service in which tourists compare their expectations with the perceived service that has been received (Brady & Robertson, 2001; Gronroos, 1984). This study will define perceived quality as the performance of the actual outcome only – as toward satisfaction of tourists. Next variable is perceived value. Woodruff, (1997) considered that value concepts differ according to the circumstances in which customers think about value (i.e., customers could perceive value different before and after purchase). Perceived value is defined as the consumer's overall assessment of the utility of a product (or service) based on perceptions of what is received (results and desired benefits) and what is given (money, effort, time) (Zeithaml, 1988). In this study, the author will define value as a facet of destination image, and not as a separate global construct that is sometimes done it the literature (Boulding et al., 1993; Baloglu & McCleary, 1999). As mentioned above, how do perceived quality and perceived value influenced to tourist satisfaction and loyalty? When consumer used product/service and compared prior expectations with perceived performance. If the performance is over expectations, a positive disconfirmation will be produced and an increase in satisfaction level will be expected (Rojas & Camarero, 2006). From tourist satisfaction with destination, they have trended to loyalty with this product/service by return and recommend to others.

2.5 Facets of tourist destination

A tourist destination is a city, town or other area the economy of which is dependent to a significant extent on the revenues accruing from tourism. It may contain one or more tourist attractions. (http://www.wordiq.com/definition/Tourist_destination).

Following the other approach, a tourist destination can be defined as an amalgam of tourism products and services consumed under the same brand name offering consumers an integrated experience, which is subjectively interpreted according to the consumers' travel itinerary, cultural background, purpose of visit, past experience etc. (Buhalis, 2000; Fuchs & Weiermair, 2003). Tourism products and services such as accommodation, travel, food, entertainment, etc. (V. Zabkar et al., 2010). In the tourism context, Lew, (1987) considered that those attractions are the elements of a destination that attract tourists, such as scenery to be seen, environment to be perceived (e.g., weather, public hygiene), activities to take part in, and experiences to remember. To be precise, the attractions provide the motivations and the magnetism necessary to persuade an individual to visit a determined place (Alhemoud & Armstrong, 1996).

Base on previous studies, in this study, factors influencing tourist destination were classified into five dimensions, involving environment, infrastructure & accessibility, culture and social, tourist leisure & entertainment and local food. These facets were selected because they are the most quoted in the tourism literature (Iso-Ahola & Mannel, 1987; Cossens, 1989; Shoemaker, 1989; Fodness, 1994; Uysal, Mclellan & Syrakaya, 1996; Mohsin & Ryan, 2003). Some previous studies only make list of different attributes, and not try to categories those in facets or factors (Beerli & Martin, 2004; Chi & Qu, 2008). However, in this study, the author will try to define and discuss the most important facets of tourists destination and include the different attributes under those facets. The main facets or dimensions forming the global destination image is presented in table 2.1 follow

Table 2.1: Facets/attributes forming the destination image

Environment	Infrastructure & Accessibility	Culture and social
Beauty of the scenery	Quality of roads	Hospitality of people
Attractiveness of the city	Public transport	Friendliness of people
Islands	Hotels quality & service	Festival/events
Beaches	Restaurants quality & service	
Cleanliness	Discotheques and clubs	
Safety	Easy access to the area	
Prices of accommodation	Well communicated traffic flow	
Communication skills& services of staffs		

Tourist leisure & entertainment	Local food
Sport activities: cock-fighting, fishing, draging on, pulling canoes, so on.	Variety & uniqueness of foods
Fashionable	Quality of foods
Night life	Prices of foods
Shopping possibilities	

(Adapted from Beerli & Martin, 2004; Chi & Qu, 2008 and revised to appropriate the characteristics of Nha Trang)

2.5.1 Environment

Travel is to discover, learn about new and strange somethings or save/ remember beautiful scenery of natural. Each destination/area has their own strange beauty. For example, travellers from Northern regions and climates tend to spend a proportion of their annual holiday in the South where they can enjoy sunshine as well as sea sports. (Buhalis, 2000).

Nha Trang has advantage about location, landscape, climate and so on. All of them are created Nha Trang has more ability to develop diverse forms of tourism. Nha trang has many famous islands such as Hon Tre: with the beautiful natural beaches on most of Vietnam, temperate climate, low winds, vegetational cover is pristine; Hon Tam: a major tourist attraction island, with green carpet of tropical forest, long sandy beach, variety of sports; Hon Mun: coral abundance and diversity in Vietnam. In addition, there are Hon Lao, Hon Thi, Hon Mieu, etc. Today, Nha Trang ranks among the top of all beaches in Vietnam (Source: *http://vietwondertravel.com*). Moreover, there are many attractive places in the center city such as Dam market; Long Son pagoda –

pagoda has Buddha statues (also known as the White Buddha) is classified into Vietnam Guinness: "The temple has the largest outdoor statues of Buddha in Vietnam", with 21m high; Diamond bay – wonderful resort, so on. The city is very little pollution or noise from vehicles.

2.5.2   Infrastructure & accessibility

Infrastructure, mean those tools which are fairly transparent for most people we know about, wide in both temporal and spatial scope, embedded in familiar strutures – like power grids, water, the Internet, airlines. (Yates & Maanen, 2001, pp 305-306).

Accessibility may be defined as the easy-to-reach desired destinations by means of a specific transport system. Accessibility is of great importance both from the point of view of regional development and that of social welfare. It depends to a great extent on the building of transport infrastructures and in turn influences land use and mobility. (Gutierrez, 1987).

Nha Trang has convenient transportation with water way, road, railway and airway. Especially, Nha Trang has the largest railway station in the North-South railway line in Vietnam. This is one of the factors to make tourist visit Nha Trang. Moreover, Nha Trang is place focus on many famous hotels and resorts. For example, Vinpearl land resort is known as tourist paradise, where attractive of both domestics and international tourists. Sheraton Nha Trang is known for having a wonderful position overlooking the Nha Trang bay, in here tourists can enjoy sea and beauty of city. Diamond bay resort and spa is luxury, beautiful and magnificent place, space is quiet and peace. And so on.

2.5.3   Culture & social

Tourists drawn to a process orientation would enjoy meeting local artisans, hearing their stories, watching craft demonstrations, and learning about the cultural and historical significance for a craft in its local context. (Yu & Littrell, 2003). One of the aspects that is attracting increasing attention is the motivation of visitors to attend special events (Uysal et al., 1991; Uysal, Gahan & Martin, 1993; Mohr et al., 1993; Formica & Uysal, 1996; Crompton & McKay, 1997; Formica & Murrmann, 1998). Some researchers have focused on a single event, for instance, a country corn festival (Uysal, Gahan & Martin, 1993) and a hot-air balloon festival (Mohr et al., 1993) in South Carolina, a jazz festival in Umbria (Formica & Uysal, 1996), etc. People also travelled to cities on pilgrimage for religious purposes, as this is where all major cathedrals, mosques and temples were usually located. (Buhalis, 2000).

Nha trang was also selected to organize major events such as sea festival Nha Trang, or the beauty competition such as Viet Nam Miss, Miss world Vietnamese 2007, Miss Universe 2008, Miss Earth 2010, etc. In addition, every year, there are many traditional festivals organized in Nha Trang such as whales festival, Tower of the lady PoNagar festival is held from 20th to the 23rd of the third Lunar month, Hung temple festival on 10th day of Third Lunar month, etc. Characteristics of people in here are friendly, hospitable, hardworking.

Back in time, Khanh Hoa province is a land with rich history – culture. For example, Tower of lady PoNagar in Nha Trang city is a faith architecture of the largest in the system of Cham towers in Vietnam.

2.5.4   Tourist leisure & entertainment

According to the *Tourism Works for America 1998 Report* (Travel Industry Association of America 1998), shopping was ranked first among leisure activities by U.S. resident travelers and overseas travelers to the United States. Tourists not only invest time toward shopping during their travels, but they also spend approximately one-third of their total tourism expenditures on retail purchases (Gratton & Taylor, 1987; Littrell et al., 1994). Littrell et al., (1994) identified four tourism styles according to the tourists' preferred travel activities, souvenirs, and shopping preferences. They purchased souvenirs that symbolized their vacation destinations through a name or logo on the products. Fridgen, (1996) noted that British tourists visiting NorthAme rica ranked shopping and taking pictures as the 1st and 2nd preferred activities. Page, (1994); Law, (1993, 1996); Mazanec, (1997) researched the attractions of urban destination. They chose several important attractions as well as entertainment opportunities such as theatre, concerts, bars, restaurants, discos, etc.

Dam market is the biggest market and as well as trade symbol of Nha trang city. This is a commercial shopping center and also the tourist attractions with beautiful architecture, unique. At night, tourists can visit some places to relax, instance, Bar sailing club, Sunrise hotel bar, Yasaka dance hall, etc. Moreover, some leisure center as Diamond bay resort & golf, Hon Tam, etc had hold many sport activities for visitors.

For example: dancing, circus or traditional game: fishing, cock-fighting, draging on, so on. In addition, many games on beaches attractives tourists such as Jetkey water motorcycles, pulling canoes, water driving pedicabs, so on.

2.5.5 Local food

Hudman suggested food has become an increasingly important element in the tourist industry and up to 25% of total tourist expenditure is accounted for by foods and this number is even much higher (Hudman, 1986). Recently, in the literature on tourist destinations, more and more researchers focus on the role of food in culture and tourism (Williams, 1997; Hegarty & O'Mahony, 2001). Food has been regarded as not only being a basic necessity for tourist consumption but also an essential element of regional culture (Jones & Jenkins, 2002). Different kinds of food is the main purpose for tourists to travel. Food can at least provide extra opportunities for tourists to be in a more memorable and enjoyable holiday atmosphere than they expected (Quan & Wang, 2004). In tourism, food as the extension of the ontological home comfort, constitutes a 'psychological island of home'. For destination food suppliers, it is necessary to understand tourists' food culture such as their eating habits, and make sure the foods used in catering are in congruous with tourists' habits and customs. Learning about the cultural differences in tourists' eating habits will effectively help improve the food service and enhance the customer satisfaction. (Quan & Wang, 2004).

Nha Trang foods are always fresh and excellent quality. If visitors want to eat fresh seafoods, visitors can choose freely them at the artifical lake after they were caught from the sea. Abalone, shrimp, squid, crab, lobster and oysters have much in other locations but they may be not fresh and delicious as here. With high nutritional value, this seafoods were processed to many kinds of foods. Specially, Salangane's nest – famous food in Nha Trang, including a lot of amino acid would bring to body the strong force for health.

2.6 Variety seeking and tourists satisfaction

More recent research in the literature on tourist satisfaction focuses on the characteristics of tourism in relation to other services and their influence on the conceptualization and measurement of satisfaction. According to Chi & Qu, (2008) more research is required to examine variables other, motivational factors than satisfaction in order to improve understanding of loyalty.

There are many definition variety seeking in different ways. Following McAlister & Pessemier, (1982), there are two kinds of varied behavior, including derived variety-seeking behavior and direct variety-seeking behavior. Derived variety-seeking was related to some other motivation not a desire for variety and this type appeared as a result of 'multiple needs, multiple users or multiple situations'. Direct variety-seeking behavior was the result of intrapersonal motives: when a person wants to satisfy her/his desire for change or novelty or satiation with product attributes, she/he does not want to remain loyal to just one, she/he prefers diversity of choice that is called variety-seeking. This study will analyze variety-seeking to find that most of the international tourists visited Nha Trang referred to derived variety-seeking behavior or direct variety-seeking behavior or both.

The search for variety in destinations and services is typical of the tourism consumer, influencing behaviour patterns and therefore behavioural loyalty (Niininen et al., 2004). Barroso et al., (2007) reported that the intensity of the relationship between satisfaction and intention to recommend and revisit is moderated by the tourist need for variety. Therefore, we consider that the variety search is a variable which can modify the intensity of the relationship between satisfaction and intentional loyalty (Valazquez et al., 2011). This study will explore the impact of variety seeking on tourist satisfaction.

2.7 Demographic characteristics and tourist satisfaction/ loyalty

The service literature also contains contributions which analyze the relationship between consumer demographic characteristics and loyalty (Lymberopolus et al., 2004; Wood, 2004; Ndubisi, 2006). For example, older consumers have less behaviour change intention (Wood, 2004); women show higher levels of loyalty in services than men (McColl-Kennedy et al., 2003). According to Patterson, (2007), younger consumers and housewives are more loyal to travel agencies. Moreover, Husbands, (1989) investigated the relationship between perception of tourism and sociodemographic variables and found that perception among Livingstone, Zambia locals differed significantly based on only age and education variables. Nickel & Wertheimer, (1979) studied the effects of age, education, occupation, income, marital status, and size of the family on consumer images of drugstores and found that age was the only variable affecting the process. Stern & Krakover, (1993) chose education level as one of the most important consumer characteristics and investigated the effects of education level of individuals on the relationship between cognitive, affective, and overall image. Based on previous research, in this study, the author will choose some factors to analysis as gender, age, nation, level of education and household income.

2.8 The conceptual model

Destination image is in this study defined as perceived quality of different facets of a city destination (Nha Trang). It is also measured as a global evaluation of quality.

Customer satisfaction is estimated with a global evaluation, which measures the overall satisfaction (Fornell, 1992; Spreng & Mackoy, 1996; Bigné et al., 2001). Additionally, the global perception about the outcome alone, the degree of satisfaction can be evaluated through specific service attributes (Mai & Ness, 2006). In tourism research, similar approach is adopted and tourist loyalty intention is represented in terms of the intention to revisit the destination and the willingness to recommend it to friends and relatives (Oppermann, 2000; Bigné et al., 2001; Chen & Gusoy, 2001; Cai et al., 2003; Niininen et al., 2004; Petrick, 2004). Therefore, intentional loyalty indicates two dimensions: revisiting intention and willingness to recommend.

To the end, this study presents the conceptual model about destination image/perceived quality – satisfaction – intention to revisit and recommend to others in tourism (show in figure 2.1). In addition, to this general conceptual model (e.g, Valazques et al., 2011), the model also include variety seeking and demographic characteristics as presented in Figure 2.2.

In testing the basic model, it is assumed that the relationship between evaluation of destination image/perceived quality, satisfaction and intentional loyalty is positive. Variety seeking is suggested to have a positive impact on satisfaction. It is reasonable to expect that some of the demographic variables are related to satisfaction and intentional loyalty.

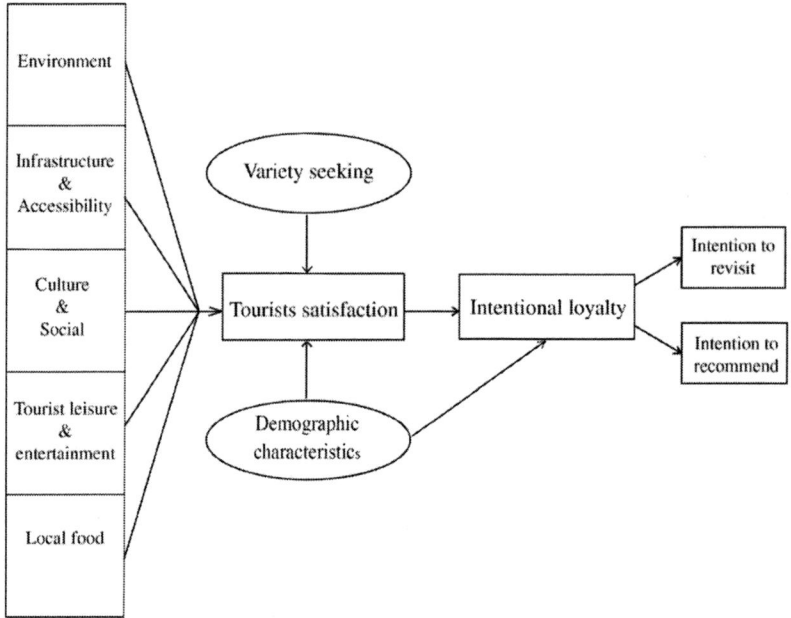

Figure 2.2 The conceptual model of this study

Chapter 3

METHODOLOGY

The purpose of this chapter is to present the process of collecting data and analysis methods. The research investigate which attributes satisfy tourists who visiting Nha Trang by surveying international visitors. This thesis use primary data from survey for the analysis. The study selected Nha Trang city as the study area to accomplish this thesis because Nha Trang is one of the most famous tourism destination in Vietnam. Due to its variety and year attractiveness of city. In 2010, more than 350,000 internatinal tourists come to visit. To accomplish this thesis, a model was designed, shown in figure 2.2. Facets/ attributes forming destination image shown in table 2.1.

3.1 Sample and data collection

First, the survey instrument was revised, and pre-testing of the questionnaire. 10 respondents were asked to complete a form questionnaire. Based on the feedback received, the questionnaire was modified and a final questionnaire was completed. The purpose of the pretest was to validate the questions of the study.

Data was collected from international tourists in Nha Trang. Respondents were informed about the purpose of the research before they were received the questionnaire. The questions in the questionnaire are designed based on a review of the theories and specific characteristics of Nha Trang. The process of collecting data was divided to two groups. First group, including 100 questionnaires were delivered to 4 hotels, named Ocean, Anamadara, Sunrise, Yasaka for hotel guests to complete the questionnaire. Second group, including 150 questionnaires were given to four students in the Department of Tourism Management at Nha Trang University interviewing international tourists at restaurants and coffee bar, where most of the foreign tourists are focused and Nha Trang beach. 250 questionnaires were delivered to tourists at random from 30th March to 10th April, 2011. 201 questionnaires were returned in an usable quality, account for 80.4 % of total given questionnaires.

3.2 Measurement of variables

3.2.1. Travel behavior

The travel behavior was measured by past experience of visitors has with Nha Trang. For example, by asking the respondents: "How many times have you visited Nha Trang during the last 10 years?". The respondents were given on a scale from 1 time to over 10 times. "How long time have you intended to stay this time?". To be measured by a nine-point scale, 1 = 1-2 days, 2 = 3-6 days, 3 = 7-10 days, 4 = 11-14 days, 5 = 15-20 days, 6 = 3-5 weeks, 7 = 6-9 weeks, 8 = 10 weeks, 9 = more 10 weeks. "What kind of accommodation are your mostly staying this year?". The tourists were asked to indicate the level of experience they are familiar with Nha Trang.

3.2.2. Destination image – facets and attributes

The 25 items of attributes were adapted from Beerli & Martin, (2004), Chi & Qu, (2008) and revised to appropriate the characteristics of Nha Trang (Table 2.1). The attributes/aspects destination were measured using a single 7-point Semantic-differential type scale, ranged from "very bad" (1) to "very good" (7) and a neutral score at middle of 4. The respondents were asked to score to each of the 25 attributes (see Appendix 2.1 for this part of the questionnaire).

3.2.3. Perceived quality

A final question in this section was asked to indicate their perceived quality or general attractiveness (destination image) of Nha Trang. A 7-point Semantic-differential scale was constructed of the five items, based on the work of Walmsley & Jenkins, (1993). This scale is intended to be quite similar as the satisfaction scale discussed below, but will be used in a separate study to test its validity against satisfaction. The respondents were asked to rate "how you feel the general attractiveness of Nha Trang city", varying from 1 (dull/ unattractive/ negative/ bad/ distressing) to 7 (exiting/ attractive/ positive/ good/ relaxing).

3.2.4. Satisfaction

The scale to measure satisfaction based on Oliver, (1997), Quintal & Polczynski, (2011) and revised to fit the characteristics of Nha Trang. In literature, satisfaction is measured by eight items. Each of eight statements are measured on using a single 7-point Likert-type scale by asking respondents with questions such as "I really enjoyed the visit", "I am satisfied with my decision to visit Nha Trang", "I prefer this destination", "I have positive feelings regarding Nha Trang", "This experience is exactly what I need", "My choice to purchase this trip was a wise one", "This was a pleasant visit", "This visit was better than expected". This scale ranged from "strongly disagree" (1) to "strongly agree" (7).

3.2.5. Intention to revisit

In this study, intention to revisit was evaluated with four items such as "I plan to visit Nha Trang", "I want to visit Nha Trang", "I expect to visit Nha Trang" and "I desire to visit Nha Trang". The measures indicate how likely the respondent will choose to visit Nha Trang within 3 years. Each of four statements were using a single 7-point Likert-type scale. This scale ranged from "very unlikely" (1) to "very likely" (7). It adapted from Oliver, (1997), Kozak & Rimmimgton, (2000), and revised to suitable the characteristics of Nha Trang, by asking the respondents.

3.2.6. Recommendation

Recommendation the destination to others (friends and relative) are measured by four items. Each of four statements were using a single 7-point Likert-type scale. This scale ranged from from "strongly disagree" (1) to "strongly agree" (7). It adapted from Oliver, (1997), Kozak & Rimmimgton, (2000), Wnag & Hsu, (2010) and revised to suitable the characteristics of Nha Trang, by asking the respondents such as "I will visit Nha Trang again in the future", "If I could have done it again, I would have chosen this destination", "I would recommend Nha Trang to others", and "I speak positive about Nha Trang to others".

3.2.7. Variety seeking

To measure the variety seeking, we based on the scale of Van Trijp et al., (1996). Moreover, the author adds some items to suitable to this study. It consists of six items and measured using a single 7-point Likert-type scale ranged from "strongly disagree" (1) to "strongly agree" (7). The respondents were presented the assertions such as "I like to visiting many different destinations", "I prefer to go to destinations I have not visit before", "I do not usually change destination I visit from time to time", "I would like to return to a destination I am familiar with", "I am curious about new destinations I am not familiar with", and "I find myself visiting the same places time after time I am travelling".

3.2.8. Demographic characteristics

Demographics characteristics refer to gender, age, level of education, social class and country of origin (proposed by Beerli & Martin, 2004). Following Quintal & Polczynski, (2011) refer to gender, residency status, age, purpose of travel and income. And so on. Based on the result of previous studies, in this study, demographics characteristics measurement with 5 items, including gender, age, country, level of education and incomes. The questions in this part was asked respondent to indicate their view such as: "What is your gender?", "What year were you born?", "Where do you live?", "What is your highest completed education?", "What is your approximate total income in your household?". The categories of level of education ranged from lower education to Post-graduate. The categories of income ranged from Less $20,000 to $80,000 and over.

A copy of the questionnaire is attached in the appendix.

3.3 Data analysis

The collected data, after sorting out the invalid questionnaire, were coded and analyzed using Statistical Package for Social Sciences (SPSS 16.0) and Amos 16.0 software. The methods for analysis used are described in the following.

3.3.1. Exploratory factor analysis and test of reliability

Exploratory factor analysis was performed in order to select the most appropriate items for the confirmatory model: to reduce a set of multivariate observations into a set of variables (called factors) to make them more meaningful (Hair, 1998). Principal component analysis (the most common form of factor analysis) was applied with rotation (varimax) to test the convergent validity and factor loadings of items (Hair et al, 1995).

Bartlett's Test of Sphericity and Kaiser-Meyer-Olkin Measure of Sampling Adequacy (KMO) are used to determine the factorability of the data (Pallant, 2005). Items of factors are retained only if a factor loading greater than or equal 0.5, $0.5 =< KMO <= 1$ (Hoang Trong & Mong Ngoc, 2005, p.262). Bartlett test of sphericity suggest the probability is less than 0.05 (Pallant, 2005). Reliability analysis for each of the factor was obtained using the calculation of a Cronbach a coefficient. Value of Cronbach's alpha of 0.6 is the 'criterion-in-use' (Nunnally, 1978; Peterson, 1994).

3.3.2. Descriptive analysis

The purposes of this study were presented not only to find relationships among constructs in the model, but also to investigate effect factors to evaluate Nha Trang as a destination, intentional loyalty toward intention to revisit and recommend to others. In the study, a description of the variety seeking and five facets/attributes of destination image related to evaluate Nha Trang as a destination were not included into model tests. However, it is presented to understand other aspect of the scales. Descriptive statistics were carried out using SPSS 16.0.

Two-tailed Independent t-test and One-way Analysis of Variance (ANOVA) were used to identify the mean differences of satisfaction by demographic characteristics of the respondents and identify the demographic characteristics differences influenced to loyalty intention to revisit and recommendation.

3.3.3. Confirmatory factor analysis and testing of the structural relationships

CFA was used in this study to confirm the convergent validity, discriminate validity and to test appropriate constructs in the conceptual model in figure 2.2. Convergent validity is tested by the standardized factor loading. Composite reliability and variance extracted measure for each construct were calculated via a standardized factor loading and measurement error for the each indicator (Hair at el, 1995). An acceptable value for composite reliability is above 0.7 and the variance extracted is exceed 0.5 (Fornell & Larcker, 1981 and Hair et al., 1998).

In addition, to examine the discriminant validity, adopted a recommended by Fornell & Larcker, 1981. If the squared correlation between the two constructs is less than the amount of variance extracted from two constructs, the discriminant validity was upheld.

Moreover, some indexes will be used to assess overall model fit such as: Chi-square (χ2), χ2/d.f ratio, Goodness – of – fit index (GFI), Comparative fit index (CFI), Root mean square error of approximation (RMSEA). The $\chi2/d.f.$ ratio of less than 5 is used as the common decision rule of an acceptable overall model fit (Chen & Chen, 2010). Following the recommendation of Hair et al., (1998), an acceptable model fits are indicated that the values for Comparative fit index (CFI), and Goodness of fit index (GFI) were greater than 0.9; values for Root mean square error of approximation (RMSEA) were less than 0.08 represent a moderate fit, while values less than 0.05 are close fit (Browne & Cudeck, 1992). In this study, the author uses the value of Chi-square, $\chi2/d.f.$ ratio, GFI, CFI and RMSEA to test the Goodness of Fit of the models.

After confirming convergent validity and discriminant validity by measurement models, Structural Equation Modeling (SEM) were estimated to test the relationship among constructs.

Chapter 4

RESULTS

This chapter present the empirical study results and analysis from primary data collection of 201 samples. The results will be presented into five major section. The first section presents the sample with travel behavior and demographics characteristics of the respondents. The second section presents the results of the exploratory factor analysis, and the third section presents the results of the descriptive analysis to achieve the first purpose of the study. The four section presents the results of confirmatory factor analysis and reliability and the structural equation modeling of destination image and tourist satisfaction. The finally section show the results of confirmatory factor analysis and reliability and the structural model of age, the perceived quality, satisfaction and intention relationships.

4.1. Travel behavior and demographic characteristics of the respondents

During the last 10 years, almost 84.6% of the respondents visited Nha Trang 1 to 2 times. Whereas, 7% of the respondents visited Nha Trang 3 to 4 times and 8.4% rest of the respondents visited 5 times or more. Most of the respondents intented to stay for 3 to 6 days (55%), followed by group of of the respondents intented to stay for 1 to 2 days (26.7%). 18.3% rest of the respondents stayed for 6 days or more. Lastly, the great majority of an internaional visitors stayed at hotel (70.3%), following by stayed at guesthouse (23.3%), only 6.4% stayed at rent or private.

General, the results show that the dominant age group of respondents was 18 to 35 years old (80.1%), followed by 56 years and older (13.4%) and the smallest group made up 6.5% of the respondents was 36 to 55 years. These results indicate that international tourists visited Nha Trang was young. The gender distribution of the respondents was 52.7% male tourists, higher than proportion of female tourists (47.3%). The majority of respondents visited Nha Trang in the first 2011 reported that they came from the United Kingdom, account for 21.4%, followed by Australia and France with 13.4% and 11.4% respectively.

Regard to level education of respondents, 46.3% of the respondents had a university education level; 23.9% of the respondents had a high school education; 17.9% of the respondents had a college education; 10.4% of the respondents had a post-graduate education and only 1.5% of the respondents had a lower education. This results indicate that the education level of tourists visited Nha Trang was quite high.

With household income of respondents, the largest group included US $40,000 to US $59,999 (27.4%), followed by US $60,000 to US $79,999 (20.4%), US $20,000 to US $39,999 and US $80,000 and more with 18.9% and 17.4% respectively, and 15.9% of the respondents had an annual household income of less US $20,000 (Table 4.1). However, comparing income across nations are difficult because each country has different standards of living, social welfare and tax policy.

Table 4.1 Demographic characteristics of the respondents (n = 201)

Variable	Frequency	Percentage (%)
Age (years)		
18 – 35	161	80.1
36 – 55	19	9.5
> 55	21	10.4
Gender		
Male	106	52.7
Female	95	47.3
Nationality		
United Kingdom	43	21.4
Australia	27	13.4
France	23	11.4
America	18	8
Germany	14	7
Ireland	11	5.5
Other countriesa	36	33.3
Level of education		
Primary school	3	1.5
High school	48	23.9
College	36	17.9
University	93	46.3
Post-graduate	21	10.4
Total household income (USD)		
Less $20,000	32	15.9
$20,000 - $39,999	38	18.9
$40,000 - $59,999	55	27.4
$60,000 - $ 79,999	41	20.4
$80,000 - more	35	17.4

[a] *Comprises: Canada, Estonia, Denmark, Netherland, Holland, Malaysia, Thailand, Norway, Japan.*

4.2. Exploratory factor analysis and reliability test

Before performing the descriptive analysis, the author did an exploratory factor analysis in order to reduce the number of items/attributes in the descriptive study, as well as performing the confirmatory factor analysis. The exploratory factor analysis was performed in SPSS with varimax rotation on tourists responses for the items destination image and then for the items other construct (perceived quality, variety seeking, satisfaction, intention to revisit and recommendation).

4.2.1. Factor analysis of destination image

An exploratory factor analysis for items that the five factors with 18 variables were defined by the original 25 variables and labeled based on the core variables. Attributes with loading factors less than 0.5, loadings lower than 0.4 and with loadings higher than 0.4 on more than one factor were eliminated (Chi & Qu, 2008). The five factors included local foods, environment, infrastructure & accessibilty, culture & social, tourist leisure & entertainment. The Kaiser-Meyer-Olkin (KMO) measure of sampling adequacy is 0.81, which is goodness fit. The Bartlett's Test of Sphericity is 1.391E3, the significance of the correlation matrix (p-value) is 0.000. This number indicate that data for exploratory factor analysis to perform. Five factor selected for further analysis explained of 63.88% of cumulative variance of the data.

The selected items/attributes also have slightly high reliability value, the Cronbach alpha ranged from 0.66 to 0.82 (table 4.2), more than 0.6 by followed recommend of Peterson (1994). The high intercorrelation between the attributes (factor reliability) makes it possible to threat the attributes as reflective indicators of the different dimensions of destination image/quality.

Table 4.2 Factor statistics/ loadings of destination image

Attributes	Factor loading				
	Factor 1	Factor 2	Factor 3	Factor 4	Factor 5
Factor 1: *Local foods*					
Variety & uniqueness of foods	0.90				
Quality of foods	0.85				
Price of foods	0.81				
Shopping possibilities	0.61				
Factor 2: *Environment*					
Islands		0.84			
Beach		0.81			
Attractiveness of city		0.69			
Beauty of scenery		0.65			
Factor 3: *Infrastructure & Accessibilty*					
Quality of roads			0.90		
Public transport			0.77		
Easy access to the area			0.56		
Factor 4: *Culture & social*					
Friendliness of people				0.85	
Hospitality of people				0.84	
Cultural events/ festival				0.72	
Factor 5: *Tourist leisure & entertainment*					
Sport activities					0.81
Discotheques and clubs					0.69
Nigh life					0.51
Fashionable					0.50
Variance (%)	30.92	11.31	8.43	7.32	5.89
Cumulative variance (%)	30.92	42.23	50.66	57.99	63.88
Cronbach's Alpha	0.82	0.76	0.66	0.81	0.75

Note: Extraction Method: Principal Component Analysis
            Rotation Method: Varimax with Kaiser Normalization
            KMO (Kaiser-Meyer-Olkim Measure of Sampling Adequacy) = 0.81
            Bartlett's Test of Sphericity: $p = 0.000$ ($x2 = 1.391E3$, $df = 153$)

4.2.2. Factor analysis of the general conceptual model

The factor analyses were conducted for the items related perceived quality, variety seeking, satisfaction, intention to revisit and recommendation. The Kaiser-Meyer-Olkin (KMO) measure of sampling adequacy is 0.87, which is goodness fit. The Bartlett's Test of Sphericity is 2.494E3, the significance of the correlation matrix (p-value) is 0.000. This number indicate that data for exploratory factor analysis to perform.

Principal components analysis started with 27 items. However, the result of reliability analysis of variety seeking factor are not fit, the alpha coefficients is 0.47, less than 0.5 and 3 items out of 6 items of variety seeking have total correlation are lower than 0.3, thus 3 items are eliminated from analysing. In addition, 5 items in satisfaction factor with loading factors less than 0.5 and 1 item in recommendation with loading factors more than 1.00 were removed from the scale.

There are 18 items covering the five constructs were selected for further analysis. Those items/factors explained of 75.86% of cumulative variance of the data. The results of the factor analysis has presented in the table 4.3

Table 4.3 Factor statistics/ loadings of the general conceptual model

Attributes	Factor loading				
	Factor 1	Factor 2	Factor 3	Factor 4	Factor 5
Perceived quality					
Bad/Good	0.83				
Negative/Positive	0.81				
Unattractive/Attractive	0.76				
Distressing/Relaxing	0.74				
Dull/ Exiting	0.70				
Satisfaction					
This was a pleasant visit		0.83			
This experience is exactly what I need		0.82			
I have positive feelings regarding Nha Trang		0.71			
Intention to revisit					
I plan to visit Nha Trang			0.92		
I expect to visit Nha Trang			0.91		
I want to visit Nha Trang			0.71		
I desire to visit Nha Trang			0.68		
Variety seeking					
I like to visiting many different destinations				0.91	
I prefer to go to destinations I have not visit before				0.91	
I am curious about new destinations I am not familiar with				0.52	
Recommendation					
I would recommend Nha Trang to others					0.65
I speak positive about Nha Trang to others					0.56
If I could have done it again, I would have chosen this destination					0.61
Variance (%)	41.07	14.36	8.96	7.40	4.07
Cumulative variance (%)	41.07	55.43	64.38	71.79	75.86
Cronbach's Alpha	0.87	0.85	0.89	0.74	0.90

Note: Extraction Method: Principal Component Analysis
Rotation Method: Varimax with Kaiser Normalization
KMO (Kaiser-Meyer-Olkim Measure of Sampling Adequacy) = 0.87
Bartlett's Test of Sphericity: p = 0.000 (x2 = 2.494E3, df = 153)

4.3. Descriptive analysis about evaluation of Nha Trang as a destination

The first purpose of this study is to find how visitors evaluate the quality of different facets or attributes of a destination image of Nha Trang, how satisfied they are with Nha Trang, loyalty intention to revisit and willingness to recommend Nha Trang to others. Thus showing the following results of descriptive analysis is to fulfill this purpose and to evaluate Nha Trang as a tourism destination. The mean value of tourists for the environment, local food, infrastructure & accessibilty, culture & social, and tourist leisure & entertainment were presented to evaluate of Nha Trang.

4.3.1. Perceived quality of the different facets of destination image

Table 4.4 show the mean value of tourists for five facets/dimensions and the corresponding attributes of destination image. The mean values indicated that the most attractiveness value is local food, followed by environment and culture & social. And the less attractiveness value was tourist leisure & entertainment and infrastructure & accessibilty. The tourists were reported that the local food related to quality of foods, variety & uniqueness of foods and stable prices of foods to be the most interesting to attract tourists visiting Nha Trang (the average mean value was 5. 33 on a scale from 1-7). Moreover, they also reported that environment factor related to beauty of scenery, travel islands, beaches and attractiveness of city and culture & social retated to events/festivals, friendliness and hospitality of people to be slightly attractiveness to evaluate Nha Trang as a destination (the average mean value was 5.27 and 5.05 respectively), but not much interesting as the local food.

In addition, the average mean value of the infrastructure & accessibilty was 4.78 and the average mean value of the tourist leisure & entertainment was 4.72. It means that both of these factors were evaluated to perform less quality and value assocated with Nha Trang as a destination. It is important to note that all these constructs in table 4.4 have been measured on a 7-point Likert scale.

Table 4.4 Mean value of the evaluation of destination image

Variables	Mean (SD)
Environment	
Beauty of scenery	5.43 (1.0)
Attractiveness of city	4.78 (1.2)
Islands	5.20 (1.1)
Beaches	5.68 (1.1)
Local food	
Quality of foods	5.44 (1.2)
Variety & uniqueness of foods	5.34 (1.2)
Prices of foods	5.21 (1.3)
Infrastructure & Accessibilty	
Public transport	4.41 (1.2)
Easy access to the area	5.23 (1.3)
Quality of roads	4.70 (1.4)
Culture & social	
Friendliness of people	5.44 (1.3)
Hospitality of people	5.27 (1.3)
Cultural events/ festival	4.45 (1.1)
Tourist leisure and entertainment	
Fashionable	4.63 (1.1)
Night life	5.00 (1.2)
Shopping possibilities	4.74 (1.1)
Sport activities	4.42 (1.1)
Discotheques and clubs	4.81 (1.3)

4.3.2. How satisfied are international visitors with Nha Trang

Satisfaction was measured by eight items. Each of eight statements are measured on using a single 7-point Likert-type scale by asking respondents. This scale ranged from "strongly disagree" (1) to "strongly agree" (7). Because the results are almost similar, the author selected to report the frequencies of item "This was a pleasant visit" which reported the highest factor loadings.

The results in table 4.5 shows that among tourists visiting Nha Trang, majority of the respondents in this study were evaluated their feeling to pleasant as slightly agree to strongly agree for the satisfaction (84.6%). In average the respondents were evaluated that their feeling is better to visit Nha Trang (5.52). The results shows that the highest percent of the respondents are slightly agree (35.3%), it means slightly satisfaction, following percent of the respondents are neutral. While the percent of the respondents are strongly agree to satisfied to be 19.4%. It explains that tourists may have not strong satisfaction with visiting Nha Trang.

Table 4.5 Tourists' satisfaction with visiting Nha Trang (% of sample)

Items	1	2	3	4	5	6	7	Average
This was a pleasant visit Nha Trang	1.0	0.0	3.5	10.9	29.9	35.3	19.4	5.52

Table 4.6 show the mean difference between satisfaction and demographic characteristics of the respondents (Two-tailed Independent t-test and One-way ANOVA). The results analysis indicated that no significant difference in tourists satisfaction was found by gender, education level and household income. Significant difference in the satisfaction of the international tourists were found by age (F = 2.53, p = 0.082 < 0.1). The results about age explained that over 55 years old group were the most satisfied with Nha Trang (the mean value was 5.83). Followed by 18-35 years old group and the 36-55 years old group are slightly satisfied with Nha Trang (the mean value was 5.27 and 5.22 respectively), but not much satisfied as over 55 years old group.

Table 4.6 The mean difference between satisfaction and demographic characteristics of the respondents (Two-tailed Independent t-test and One-way ANOVA)

Variable	Frequency	Mean
Age (years) ($F = 2.53^*$)		
18 – 35	161	5.27
36 – 55	19	5.22
> 55	21	5.83
Gender ($F = 0.73$)		
Male	106	5.23
Female	95	5.43
Level of education ($F = 1.29$)		
Lower education	3	6.11
High school	48	5.19
College	36	5.30
University	93	5.30
Post-graduate	21	5.71
Total household income (USD) ($F = 0.39$)		
Less $20,000	32	5.27
$20,000 - $39,999	38	5.34
$40,000 - $59,999	55	4.41
$60,000 - $ 79,999	41	5.16
$80,000 - more	35	5.41

Note: Satisfaction mean ranges from 1 (strongly disagree) to 7 (strongly agree)
   * $p < 0.1$

4.3.3. Loyalty intention and recommendation

Intention to revisit was measured with 4 items by asking respondents plan/ want/ expect and desire to visit Nha Trang within 3 years on a 7-point Likert scale, ranged from (1) very unlikely to (7) very likely. Because high correlations between those items and the results are almost similar, the author use only one item (e.g, expect to visit Nha Trang) to report frequencies. The same precedure is used for recommendation were "recommend" to other is used as the only item.

Regarding to intention to revisit, the results in table 4.7 shows that the highest percent of the respondents were very unlikely expect to visit Nha Trang within 3 years (25.4%). Following percent of the respondents were neutral, while the percent of the respondents were very likely to be 7.5%. It explains that tourists may have not strong intention to revisit Nha Trang. In average the respondents were evaluated that the intention to revisit Nha Trang was under medium (3.61), very low.

Table 4.7 Intention to revisit and recommend Nha Trang to other (% of sample)

Items	Very unlikely		Neutral estimation			Very likely		Average
	1	2	3	4	5	6	7	
I expect to visit Nha Trang within three years	25.4	10.9	9.5	14.9	17.9	13.9	7.5	3.61
I would recommend Nha Trang to others	0.5	1.5	3.0	12.9	17.4	36.3	28.4	5.68

Within the recommendation Nha Trang to others were measured with four items and measured in a 7-point Likert scale. The results in table 4.7 shows that the highest percent of the respondents were slightly agree to recommend Nha Trang to others (36.3%). Following percent of the respondents were strongly agree to recommend to be 28.4%. It explains that tourists may have strongly agree to recommend Nha Trang to others. In average the respondents were evaluated that the recommendation Nha Trang to others was high (5.68).

Table 4.8 show the mean difference between intention to revisit, intention to recommend and demographic characteristics of the respondents (Two-tailed Independent t-test and One-way ANOVA). The results analysis indicated that no significant difference in recommendation was found by age, gender, education level and household income. And similar results in intention to revisit. However, only age was significant difference in loyalty intention to revisit. The results explained that over 55 years old group had the most intented to revisit Nha Trang (the mean value was 5.44). Followed by 36-55 years old group neutral to intented to revisit Nha Trang (the mean value was 4.90). The results indicates that 18-35 years old group had no intented to revisit Nha Trang.

Table 4.8 The mean difference between intention to revisit, intention to recommend and demographic characteristics of the respondents (Two-tailed Independent t-test and One-way ANOVA)

Variable		Intention to revisit		Intention to recommend	
	Frequency	Mean	F	Mean	F
Age (years)			12.34*		2.28
18 – 35	161	3.87		5.48	
36 – 55	19	4.90		5.91	
> 55	21	5.44		5.9	
Gender			0.01		0.23
Male	106	4.34		5.6	
Female	95	3.894		5.52	
Level of education			0.81		0.96
Lower education	3	4.60		6.22	
High school	48	3.92		5.37	
College	36	4.48		5.48	
University	93	4.02		5.64	
Post-graduate	21	4.42		5.70	
Total household income (USD)			1.26		1.80
Less $20,000	32	3.55		5.18	
$20,000 - $39,999	38	4.32		5.79	
$40,000 - $59,999	55	4.23		5.44	
$60,000 - $ 79,999	41	4.23		5.62	
$80,000 - more	35	4.17		5.79	

Note: Intention to revisit and intention to recommend mean ranges from 1 (strongly disagree) to 7 (strongly agree)
       * p < 0.1

In general, the results may explain that among tourists felt satisfied, they have intented to recommed higher than to revisit.

All items of demographic characteristic chose for analyzing in model, there are only age had influenced to satisfaction of tourists (F = 2.53, p = 0.082) and intention to revisit (F = 12.34, p = 0.000); these characteristics rest are not related to satisfaction and intention to revisit. Moreover, all demographic characteristic chose for analyzing are not related to recommendation. Thus, I will only include age as the only demographic variable in testing the final conceptual model

4.4. Explaining destination image and tourist satisfaction relationship

This section is to explore the relationship among the five facets/attributes of destination image to satisfaction of visitors visiting Nha Trang. Before performing the confirmatory factor analysis, the author performed and exploratory factor analysis of the 25 items adapted from Beerli & Martin, (2004) and Chi & Qu, (2008) to assess destination image and 8 items to assess satisfaction. From the results presented in table 4.2 and table 4.3, the each facet were selected for the confirmatory factor analysis in this study.

4.4.1. Confirmatory factor analysis and validity of the measurement

First, a confirmatory factor analysis (CFA) is used to confirm the factor loadings of the six constructs initiated with 18 items (3 items per facets/ dimension and for satisfaction) and to assess the model fit. The measurement model was evaluated by examining a battery of item reliability, construct reliability and average variance extracted (i.e., convergent validity) and distincting from each other (i.e., discriminate validity) (Joreskog & Sorbom, 1993).

Items with large residuals or standarized factor loadings less than 0.5 and cross-loading to other constructs were removed from the analysis. Thus, there are 3 items of attributes destination construct was removed from analysis. Standardized confirmatory factor analysis coefficients and construct reliability of destination image and tourists satisfaction shown in Table 4.9.

Table 4.9 Standardized confirmatory factor analysis coefficients and construct reliability of destination image and tourists satisfaction

Constructs and indicators	St. factor loadings	t-value	Composite reliability	Variance Extracted
Environment			**0.73**	**0.48**
Beauty of scenery	.72	9.99		
Attractiveness of city	.71	9.77		
Islands	.64	8.74		
Local food			**0.84**	**0.65**
Quality of foods	.92	15.48		
Variety & uniqueness of foods	.81	13.11		
Prices of foods	.66	10.06		
Infrastructure & Accessibilty			**0.76**	**0.51**
Public transport	.76	10.81		
Easy access to the area	.72	10.20		
Quality of roads	.67	9.34		
Culture & social			**0.85**	**0.66**
Friendliness of people	.90	15.12		
Hospitality of people	.85	13.88		
Cultural events/ festival	.69	10.58		
Tourist leisure and entertainment			**0.75**	**0.50**
Fashionable	.73	10.39		
Night life	.72	10.23		
Shopping possibilities	.68	9.65		
Satisfaction			**0.86**	**0.67**
I have positive feelings regarding Nha Trang	.86	14.16		
This was a pleasant visit	.83	13.55		
This experience is exactly what I need	.75	11.85		

Note: Chi – Square = 259.737, df = 120, p-value = .000; RMSEA = .076; GFI = .876; CFI = .912; N = 201

As shown in Table 4.9, t-values for all the standardized factor loadings of the items, ranging from 8.74 to 15.48, were found to be significant ($p < 0.01$). The standardized factor loadings were ranged from 0.64 to 0.92. Fornell & Larcker (1981) and Hair et al. (1998) recommended that the composite reliability should be greater than or equal to 0.70 and variance extracted should be greater than or equal to 0.50. In this study, composite reliability estimates ranging from 0.73 to 0.86 exceeded the critical value of 0.7, indicating it was satisfactory estimation. The average variances extracted for all the constructs range between 0.48 and 0.67, except constructs environment value was 0.48, less than the suggested value of 0.5. However, the study choose to keep environment value in the model because it has a positively influence on tourists satisfaction. These indicate that the measurement in the first part of model has good convergent validity. Therefore, the measurement model is reliable and meaningful to test the structural relationships among the constructs. The value for RMSEA of 0.076, were less than 0.08 (Browne & Cudeck, 1992), thus a moderate fit. The other goodness-of-fit measures with Chi - Square value ($\chi 2$) of 259.737 (df = 120, p = 0.000); GFI = 0.876 (nearly 0.9); CFI = 0.912 also showed acceptable values (higher than 0.90). This results suggest that six factors solution for confirmatory factor analysis is reliable and the first part of model fits the data quite well.

The measurement of environment, local food, infrastructure & accessibilty, culture & social, tourist leisure & entertainment and satisfaction were tested to prove discriminant validity. To examine the discriminant validity, average variance extracted value for each construct was compared with the squared correlation between that construct and other related constructs (Hatcher, 1994). If the squared correlation between the two constructs is less than the amount of variance extracted from two constructs, the discriminant validity was upheld (Fornell & Larcker, 1981).

Table 4.10 Correlations of the constructs for destination image and tourists satisfaction

	1	2	3	4	5	6
1. Environment	*1*					
2. Local food	. 43	*1*				
3. Infrastructure & Accessibilty	. 32	. 32	*1*			
4. Culture & Social	. 38	. 46	. 47	*1*		
5. Tourist leisure & Entertainment	. 43	. 53	. 52	. 51	*1*	
6. Satisfaction	. 52	. 46	. 38	. 45	. 45	*1*

Note: Chi – Square = 259.737, df = 120, p-value = .000; RMSEA = .076; GFI = .876; CFI = .912;

Note: - All of inter- correlations are significant at p < 0.01

       - Correlations presented below the diagonal of the matrix.

Table 4.10 shown the correlations of the constructs in the first part of model in this study. All of inter- correlations are significant at p < 0.01 and ranges are all less than 0.53. The results considered that the squared correlation between each of the constructs is less than the average variance extracted from each pair of constructs, the discriminant validity exist.

4.4.2. Structural equation analysis of the proposed relationships

The first part of model indicates that Chi - Square = 259.737 with df = 120, p-value = 0.000. As the $\chi2$ value is very sensitive to sample size, however, it frequently results in rejecting a well-fitted model when sample size increases (Chen & Chen, 2010). The $\chi2/d.f.$ ratio of less than 5 is used as the common decision rule of an acceptable overall model fit. In the model, the normed $\chi2$ is 2.146, indicating an acceptable fit. Furthermore, other indicators of goodness of fit are GFI = 0.876, can be accepted value, CFI = 0.912, RMSEA = 0.076.

The results of all paths coefficients in the first part of model are shown in Table 4.9

Table 4.11 Results of structural for destination image and tourists satisfaction

Path analysis	Estimate	t-value	Testing re-sult
Environment ➜ Satisfaction	.321	3.289**	Support
Infrastructure & Accessibilty ➜ Satisfaction	.087	.892ns	Not support
Culture & Social ➜ Satisfaction	.165	1.812*	Support
Local food ➜ Satisfaction	.164	1.800*	Support
Tourist leisure & Entertainment ➜ Satisfaction	.095	.848ns	Not support

*p < 0.1;   ** p < 0.05;   ns: non-significant
Chi - Square = 259.737, df = 120, p-value = .000; GFI = .876, CFI = .912, RMSEA = 0.076.
Satisfaction $R^2 = 0.40$

Table 4.11 shows that environment, culture & social and local food had a positive influence on satisfaction with $\beta = 0.321$, t = 3.289, p < 0.05 for environment, $\beta = 0.165$, t = 1.812, p < 0.1 for culture & social and $\beta = 0.164$, t = 1.800, p < 0.1 for local food are significantly, thereby supporting these three relationship. It may explain the tourists will feel more satisfied, if environment, culture & social and local food factors are improved and enhanced about quality of foods, level of attraction of island, scenery and city, so on.

However, the positive relationship between infrastructure & accessibilty and satisfaction is not significant ($\beta = 0.087$, t = 0.892ns), tourist leisure & entertainment had a positive effect on satisfaction is not confirmed ($\beta = 0.095$, t = 0.848ns), which are not supporting these two relationships.

There are three out of five relationship are supported. Among three factors influenced on satisfaction, environment factor carried the heaviest weight for tourist satisfaction ($\beta = 0.321$, t = 3.289, p < .005), following by culture & social factor ($\beta = 0.165$, t = 1.812, p < 0.1) and local food factor ($\beta = 0.164$, t = 1.800, p < 0.1). Those variables explained 40% of the variation in the tourists general satisfaction in visiting Nha Trang.

4.5. Explaining loyalty intention and recommendation

The final part of this study is to test the conceptual model presented in figure 2.1. and figure 2.2. Destination image is defined as a global evaluation of perceived quality of Nha Trang and demographic characteristics is limited to age (based on the results from the descriptive part above). In addition, variety seeking is included in the model together with two dimensions of intentional loyalty toward intention to revisit and intention to recommend.

4.5.1 Confirmatory factor analysis and validity of the measurement

Before performing the confirmatory factor analysis, the author performed and exploratory factor analysis of perceived quality/destination image (general measure), satisfaction, variety seeking, intention to revisit and recommendation. The results of this is presented in table 4.3. The each construct were selected for the confirmatory factor analysis in this study.

Next, a new confirmatory factor analysis (CFA) is used to confirm the factor loadings of the five constructs initiated with 16 items (5 items to measure perceived quality, 3 items to measure satisfaction, 3 items to measure variety seeking, 3 items to measure recommendation and 2 items to measure intention to revisit), to perform a new regression. The results in two items of intention to revisit were removed from analysis because of items with large residuals, factor loadings more than 1.00. Standardized confirmatory factor analysis coefficients and construct reliability of loyalty intention and recommendation shown in Table 4.12.

Table 4.12 Standardized confirmatory factor analysis coefficients and construct reliability of the latent constructs

Constructs and indicators	St. factor loadings	t-value	Composite reliability	Variance Extracted
Perceived quality			**0.88**	**0.60**
Bad/Good	.89	15.53		
Negative/Positive	.85	14.38		
Unattractive/Attractive	.73	11.60		
Distressing/Relaxing	.72	11.28		
Dull/ Exiting	.65	9.98		
Satisfaction			**0.86**	**0.66**
I have positive feelings regarding Nha Trang	.88	15.08		
This was a pleasant visit	.82	13.43		
This experience is exactly what I need	.74	11.76		
Variety seeking			**0.79**	**0.57**
I like to visiting many different destinations	.92	13.20		
I prefer to go to destinations I have not visit before	.78	11.22		
I am curious about new destinations I am not familiar with	.51	7.12		
Recommendation			**0.91**	**0.78**
I would recommend Nha Trang to others	.95	17.62		
I speak positive about Nha Trang to others	.92	16.60		
If I could have done it again, I would have chosen this destination	.76	12.46		
Intention to revisit			**0.94**	**0.89**
I expect to visit Nha Trang	.98	16.53		
I plan to visit Nha Trang	.91	14.93		

Note: Chi – Square = 149.14, df = 94, p-value = 0.000; RMSEA = 0.054; GFI = 0.92; CFI = 0.97.

As shown in Table 4.12, t-values for all the standardized factor loadings of the items, ranging from 7.12 to 17.62, were found to be significant ($p < 0.01$). The standardized factor loadings were ranged from 0.51 to 0.98. The composite reliability estimates ranging from 0.79 to 0.94, greater than to 0.70; and the average variances extracted range between 0.57 and 0.89, greater than to 0.50 following to recommend by Hair et al. (1998). These indicate that the measurement model has good convergent validity. Therefore, the measurement model is reliable and meaningful to test the structural relationships among the constructs. The value for RMSEA of 0.054, were less than 0.08 (Browne & Cudeck, 1992), thus a moderate fit. The other goodness-of-fit measures with Chi - Square value ($\chi 2$) of 149.14 (df = 94, p = 0.000); GFI = 0.92; CFI = 0.97 prove that the measurement is reliable and the last part of model fits the data very well.

The measurement of perceived quality, variety seeking, satisfaction, recommendation and intention to revisit were tested to prove discriminant validity.

Table 4.13 Correlations of the latent constructs

	1	2	3	4	5
1. Perceived quality	*1*				
2. Variety seeking	0.15	*1*			
3. Satisfaction	0.63	0.22	*1*		
4. Recommendation	0.57	0.21	0.78	*1*	
5. Intention to revisit	0.37	-0.16	0.25	0.37	*1*

Note: Chi – Square = 149.14, df = 94, p-value = 0.000; RMSEA = 0.054; GFI = 0.92; CFI = 0.97.

Note: - All of inter- correlations are significant at p < 0.01

        - Correlations presented below the diagonal of the matrix

Table 4.13 shown the correlations of the constructs of the perceived quality, variety seeking, satisfaction and intentional loyalty. All of inter- correlations are significant at p < 0.01 and ranges are all less than 0.78. The results considered that the squared correlation between each of the constructs is less than the average variance extracted from each pair of constructs, which constitutes the discriminant validity.

4.5.2 Structural model of the age, perceived quality, satisfaction and intention relationship

The model indicates that Chi - Square = 190.27 with df = 111, p-value = 0.000. The $\chi2$/d.f. ratio of is 1.7, less than 5, indicating an acceptable fit. Furthermore, other indicators of goodness of fit are GFI = 0.9, CFI = 0.96, RMSEA = 0.06.

The results of all paths coefficients in the last part of model are shown in Table 4.14

Table 4.14 Results of structural in the latent constructs

Path analysis	Estimate	t-value	Testing result
Perceived quality → Satisfaction	0.62	8.05***	Support
Variety seeking → Satisfaction	0.16	2.38**	Support
Age → Satisfaction	-0.11	-1.75*	Support
Satisfaction → Intention to revisit	0.21	2.95**	Support
Satisfaction → Recommendation	0.78	10.93***	Support
Age → Intention to revisit	-0.42	-6.32***	Support
Age → Recommendation	-0.43	-0.83ns	Not support

$*p < 0.1$; $** p < 0.05$; $*** p < 0.001$;   ns: non-significant
Chi - Square = 190.27, df = 111, p-value = 0.000; GFI = 0.9, CFI = 0.96,
RMSEA = 0.06
Satisfaction R^2 = 0.44
Recommendation R^2 = 0.62
Intention to revisit R^2 = 0.24

Perceived quality and variety seeking are significant and positive related to satisfaction with β = 0.62, t = 8.05, p < 0.001 for perceived quality; β = 0.16, t = 2.38, p < 0.05 for variety seeking, thereby supporting these two relationship. It may explain that Nha Trang city is a tourism destination which international tourists visiting here, they felt satisfied.

Age had a negative influence on satisfaction with β = - 0.11, t = - 1.75, p < 0.1 is significantly, thereby confirming this relationship. It may explain that the older people is more satisfied with visiting Nha Trang than the younger people.

Satisfaction is significant and positive related to intention to revisit (β = 0.21, t = 2.95, p < 0.05) and does show the similar relationship with recommendation (β = 0.78, t = 10.93, p < 0.001), providing supported for these two relationships. It may explain that the more satisfied tourists feel about Nha Trang, the more intend to revisit and recommend to others.

Age is significant and negative related to intention to revisit with β = -0.42, t = -6.32, p < 0.001, thereby confirming this relationship. It may explain that the older people has intention to revisit Nha Trang higher than the younger people.

However, and the negative relationship between age and recommendation is not significant with β = -0.43, t = -0.83ns, which are not supporting this relationship.

There are six out of sevent relationship are supported. The explained variance for the perceived quality, variety seeking and age were R^2 = 0.44 for satisfaction of international tourists visiting Nha Trang. Those variables explained 44% of the variation in the tourists general satisfaction in visiting Nha Trang. R^2 = 0.24 for intention to revisit Nha Trang and R^2 = 0.62 for recommendation Nha Trang to others explained that international tourists satisfied with visiting Nha Trang have 24 percent in intention to revisit Nha Trang and 62 percent in recommendation Nha Trang to others.

In conclusion, the results of confirmatory factor analysis and structural equation analysis confirmed that all items in the measurement of model reflect the theoretical constructs as we expected.

Chapter 5

DISCUSSION AND CONCLUSIONS

The main purpose of the thesis is to find how visitors evaluate the quality of different facets or attributes of a destination image of Nha Trang, how satisfied they are with Nha Trang, loyalty intention to revisit and willingness to recommend Nha Trang to others. The second is to investigate what "image" is most important to explain global satisfaction with visiting Nha Trang. As well as to investigate how perceived quality, satisfaction and other motivational or dismotivational factors (e.g., demographic characteristics, variety seeking,) influence loyalty intention to revisit and willingness to recommend to others. The survey was carried out in Nha Trang city, Vietnam and sample of 201 respondents was used. In this study, all items used to measure the constructs in the conceptual model were adopted from previous researches and revised to appropriate to characteristics of Nha Trang city, Vietnam. Techniques were conducted by SPSS 16.0 and Amos 16.0. In particular, exploratory factor analysis (EFA) is used to explore the structure of each construct; Confirmatory factor analysis (CFA) is run to test the item reliability, construct reliability and average variance extracted the measurement model; Structural equation modeling (SEM) analysis to test the proposed relationships between the constructs. The following is refered to main findings and discussion about the results, implications as well as limitations and future research.

5.1. Main findings and discussions

Both the exploratory and confirmatory factor analysis of the structure of destination image confirmed a five-factor solution: environment, local food, culture & social, infrastructure & assessibility and tourist leisure & entertainment. This is in accordance with the theoretical framework (Beerli & Martin, 2001; Chi & Qu, 2008) used in this study (see Table 2.1).

In this study, the international tourists reported that they had strongly positive interesting the local food toward visiting Nha Trang (the mean value was 5.33). Moreover, local food is found to significantly affect on satisfaction with visiting Nha Trang as a destination (coefficient = 0.16, p < 0.1). It is consistent to previous studies on food and enjoyable holiday relation (Quan & Wang 2004).

Explaining tourists satisfaction and intention to revisit Nha Trang, Vietnam   49

In addition, environment and culture & social are slightly attractiveness to tourists visiting Nha Trang (the mean value was 5.27 and 5.05 respectively). Beside that, the causual effect environment and culture & social on satisfaction are significant. It is logical and similar to previous studies (such as Crompton & McKay, 1997; Formica & Murrmann, 1998). As mentioned above, Nha Trang city is an international marine tourism center which cutural value and humanity is appreciated, environment is quite clean, a man is gentle and courteous. Moreover, the wonderful natural scenery of the bay, ocean, mountains, rivers and diverse marine ecosystems are more attractive to tourists. Although other places have natural resources, it is not enough attractive about cutural and social (source: http://www.vietnamtourism.gov.vn). Those results confirms the findings about destination image attracted Chinese tourists in Vietnam (see Truong & King, 2009).

However, the findings showed that tourist leisure & entertainment and infrastructure & accessibilty were less quality and value associated with Nha Trang (the mean value was 4.72 and 4.78 respectively). In the empirical survey, international tourists complained that they were invited with insistence and follow them. Moreover, snatch and run assets of travellers are still happened. In addition, tourism products are still limited, not satisfied tourists' need. This findings support argument of Gratton & Taylor, 1987 and Littrell et al., 1994 that tourists not only invest time toward shopping during their travels, but they also spend approximately one-third of their total tourism expenditures on retail purchases.

In paticular, this study tested which factors are most important in explaining general evaluation or satisfaction with Nha Trang as a destination. Specific, international tourists were satisfied with Nha Trang as a beauty of scenery; islands; attractiveness of city; quality of foods, variety and uniquesness of foods; festival/event, friendliness and hospitality of people in Nha Trang. However, they were not satisfied as public transport; quality of roads; nighlife; shopping in Nha Trang. This findings also seem to be accordance with the above findings. This indicates that Nha Trang seems to be a destination for those who want to discover and experience own culture characteristics, unheard-of to things and special food in Nha Trang. This results was accordance with the previous finding in the literature that explained the significant relationship between destination image and satisfaction (see Chen & Tsai, 2007).

To evaluate Nha Trang as a tourism destination, the attractiveness of local food, environment and culture & social factors are significantly better than the tourist leisure & entertainment and infrastructure & accessibilty factors. Therefore, it is good to improve fresh quality of foods; enhance and upgrade scenery, island; educate to aware citizen to behave international tourists and protect tourism environment.

As expected, the results in this study confirmed the positive relationship between destination image/perceived quality and tourists satisfaction (coefficient = 0.62, p < 0.001); and the similar relationship between satisfaction and intentional loyalty toward intention to revisit and recommendation. It is logical because if the tourists feel that the general quality of the different facets of Nha Trang is good, they are satisfied with their travel. When they are satisfied, they want to recommend Nha Trang to others and have intention to revisit Nha Trang. It is accordant with studies on satisfaction in the recent years (Kozak & Rimmington, 2000; Yoon & Uysal, 2005; Chen & Tsai, 2007; Chen & Chen, 2010).

In addition, the findings explore that variety seeking had a positive influence on satisfaction. This indicates that travellers who want to discover and find to variety that they have not experienced yet in their life before. At Nha Trang, tourists were comparing what they expected with what they experienced. They feel satisfied about this curious. Those finding is similar to previous studies of tourists (see Valazques et al., 2011).

Except for age were demographical variables not related to tourists satisfaction and intention to revisit. Those results are different from Dimitriades, (2006). Dimitriades, (2006) found no significant relationship between age and loyalty in tourism. However, this results are similar to previous studies which indicated in the literature (Wood, 2004). All demographical variables, including level education, household income, gender and age are not effected to recommendation. Only if tourists felt satisfied, they will be intention to recommend Nha Trang to others, not depend on their characteristic. This finding are different from McColl-Kennedy et al., (2003) and Patterson, (2007). In this study, age had a negative and siginificantly influence on tourists satisfaction (β = - 0.11, t = - 1.75, p < 0.1) and intention to revisit (β = -0.42, t = -6.32, p < 0.001). The results about age explained that over 55 years old group were the most satisfied with Nha Trang. Therefore this group had intented to revisit Nha Trang more than other group. It may explain that the older people is more satisfied with visiting Nha Trang and has intention to revisit Nha Trang higher than the younger people. This useful information for planners and marketers in tourism industry in Nha Trang. Because of this findings, the tourism local authority and marketers could give more strategies and policies to attract foreign tourists visit/revisit Nha Trang. For example, Nha Trang is a peaceful city, it is suitable for older or for person who like quite. However, local authority and planners should build more exciting and eventful leisure center in Nha Trang for young people or active person.

In this study, the proposed model explain 24% the variance of tourists have intented to revisit. It is suggested that in future study, other variables should be added to improve the variance explained of intented to revisit. For example, perceived value should be a good variable toward satisfaction with visiting Nha Trang and intention to revisit Nha Trang.

In summary, this study contributes to the literature on tourists satisfaction as well as intention to revisit and intention to recommend measurement. It also constributes to practices which is discussed in the following part.

5.2. Implications

Based on the findings of this study, several implications could be made to promote and increase international tourist satisfaction and intentional loyalty toward recommend to other and revisit to Nha Trang.

This study has shown that the environment, local food and cuture & social have a significant relationship with the satisfaction of tourists. This result can be useful to the tourism planners and marketers focus more on enhancing, improving and maintaining factors that contribute to tourists satisfaction. For environment, local authorities and planners should educate citizen to have a sense of protect life environment and tourism environment; behave to tourists cuturally, friendly and condescending. For local food and cuture & social, marketers should extend many kinds of tourism product such as swim underwater, climb up a mountain, casino, modern dance hall, building many shopping ward, eating and drinking, music and song place, so on. Especially, holding common people festival, eating and drinking cutural festival, classical drama. Moreover, holding many tours of island tourism and traditional village tourism.

In addition, the findings have indicated that tourist leisure & entertainment and infrastructure & accessibilty have not a significant relationship with the tourists satisfaction. For infrastructure & accessibilty, the marketers may need some effort to improving in public transport facilities, providing quality service of hotel; special events; developing tour with diversity of activities at night to attract to international tourists such as singing & dancing, theatres, camps in the countryside or music camps in ancient houses. For tourist leisure & entertainment, planners should be training a professional staff and using English fluently follow service standards in over the world. Establing a group with militia and police who can speak English fluently to solve to complain of international tourists and guarantee international tourists' safe in tourism area.

It is hoped that this results and this recommendation will be valuable information to tourism marketers and planners in Nha Trang in evaluating and giving marketing strategies and management in the future. Nha Trang will attract more foreign tourists and potential tourists from many different countries over the world.

5.3. Limitations and future research

Some limitations of this study should be discussed in following to improve in future research.

The study was carried out in Nha Trang city. Primary data had to collect from international tourists visiting Nha Trang. Sample is relatively small. Beside, at this time, Japan happened the earthquake, Tsunami. This effected to some countries in the world and tourist's psychology are afraid to travel to another country, thus the population of this study was limited to international visitors. The sample size constituted 201 respondents and they are not statistically representative to the total population in Nha Trang or Vietnam. To overcome this limitation, future research could conduct in different seasons, collect to a larger population and extend the research scope to another famous tourism city in Vietnam.

Measurements can be improved. Some questions had to be deleted in the process – excluding probability some important attributes. Future analysis should test a formative model (e.g., Beerli & Martin, 2004) where more of the attributes are included in the study.

The conceptual model of this study are also lacked some constructs, such as perceived value (e.g., Bigne et al., 2009; Chen & chen, 2010), cost (e.g., Bigne et al., 2009), perceived risk (e.g., Quintal & Polczynski, 2011). Therefore, future research can add these constructs in the model.

The future studies should apply this conceptual model of this study in a comparative examination of the segmentation with the difference nation tourists, which not practiced in this study. Because each tourist has own characteristic such as age, social classes, habit, taste, cutural, so on. This effected to evaluate and feeling of each tourist and to decide to return and recommend to others or not. This is an important issue for tourism marketers to give many strategies which can be satisfied with many kinds of tourists.

REFERENCE

Alexandris, K., Kouthouris, C. & Meligdis, A. (2006). Increasing customers' loyalty in a skiing resort: the contribution of place attachment and service quality. International Journal of Contemporary Hospitality Management, 18(5): 414–425.

Alhemoud, A. M., & Armstrong, E. G. (1996). Image of tourism attractions in Kuwait. Journal of Travel Research, Spring, 76–80.

Anderson,W., & Sullivan, M. (1993). The antecedents and consequences of customer satisfaction for firms. Marketing Science, 12, 125–143.

Baloglu, S. & Brinberg, D. (1997). Affective images of tourism destinations. Journal of Travel Research, 35(4):11-15.

Baloglu, S. & McCleary, K. W. (1999a). A model of destination image formation. Annals of Tourism Research, 26: 868–897.

Baloglu, S. & McCleary, K. W. (1999b). US international pleasure travelers' images of four mediterranean destinations: A comparison of visitors and nonvisitors. Journal of Travel Research, 38(2), 114–129.

Barroso, Castro, C., Martin Armario, E. & Martin Ruiz, D. (2007). The influence of market heterogeneity on the relationship between a destinations image and tourists' future behavior. Tourism Management, 28(1): 175–187.

Beerli, A. & Martin, D. (2004). Factors influencing destination image. Annals of Tourism Research, Vol. 31, No. 3, pp. 657– 681.

Berne´, C. (1997). Modelizacion de la poscompra: satisfaccion y lealtad. In: Mugica JM and Ruiz S (eds) El comportamiento del consumidor. Barcelona: Ariel, 163–180.

Berne´, C., Mugica, J.M. & Yague, M.J. (2001), "The effect of variety-seeking on customer retention in services". Journal of Retailing and Consumer Services, Vol. 8, pp. 335-45.

Berne´, C., Mugica, J.M. & Rivera, P. (2005). "The managerial ability to control the varied behavior of regular customers in retailing: interformat differences". Journal of Retailing and Consumer Services, Vol. 12, pp. 151-64.

Bigné, E., Sánchez, M. I. & Sánchez, J. (2001). Tourism image, evaluation variables and after purchase behaviour: Inter-relationship. Tourism Management, 22(6), 607–616.

Bigne, J.E., Mattila, A.S. & Andreu, L. (2008). The impact of experiential consumption cognition and emotions on behavioral intentions. Journal of Services Marketing, 22(4): 303–315.

Bigne, J., Isabel Sanchez & Luisa Andreu, (2009). The role of variety seeking in short and long run revisit intentions in holiday destinations.

Bitner, M.J. & Hubbert, (1994). Encounter satisfaction versus quality: the customer's voice. In Service Quality. Sage Publications: Thousand Oaks, CA; 72–94.

Bolton, R. N. & Drew, J. H. (1991). A multistage model of customers' assessments of service quality and value. Journal of Consumer Research, 17(March), 375–384.

Boulding, W., Kalra, A., Staelin, R. & Zeithaml, V. A. (1993). A dynamic process model of service quality: from expectations to behavioral intentions. Journal of Marketing Research, 30, 7–27.

Bowen, J.T. & Chen, S.L. (2001). The relationship between customer loyalty and customer satisfaction. International Journal of Contemporary Hospitality Management, 13(5): 213–217.

Brady, M.K., Robertson, C.J. & Cronin, J.J. (2001). Managing behavioral intentions in diverse cultural environments. An investigation of service quality, service value and satisfaction for American and Ecuatorian fast-food customers. Journal of International Management, 7: 129–149.

Browne, M. W. & Cudeck, R. (1992). Alternative ways of assessing model fit. Sociological Methods & Research, 21: 230 -258.

Buhalis, D. (2000). Tourism Management, 21: 97-116

Cai, L.A., Wu, B. & Bai, B. (2003). Destination image and loyalty, Cognizant Communication Corporation, 7, 153–162.

Chen, J. & Gursoy, D. (2001). An investigation of tourists' destination loyalty and preferences, International Journal of Contemporary hospitality Management, 13: 79–86.

Chen, J. & Paliwoda, S. (2004) The influence of company name in consumer variety seeking. Journal of Brand Management, 11: 219–232.

Chen, C. & Tsai, D. (2007). How destination image and evaluative factors affect behavioral intentions? Tourism Management, 28: 1115–1122.

Chen, C. (2008). Investigating structural relationships between service quality, perceived value, satisfaction, and behavioral intentions for air passengers: evidence from Taiwan. Transportation Research Part A, 42(4): 709–717.

Chen, C. & Chen, F. (2010). Experience quality, perceived value, satisfaction and behavioral intentions for heritage tourists. Tourism Management, 31: 29–35.

Chi, C. & Qu, H. (2008). Examining the structural relationship of destination image, tourist satisfaction and destination loyalty: an integrated approach. Tourism Management 29(4): 624–636.

Chon, K. (1989). "Understanding recreational travelers' motivation, attitude and satisfaction". Tourist Review, 44 (1): 3-7.

Court, B. & Lupton, R. A. (1997). Customer portfolio development:modelling destination adopters, inactives and rejecters. Journal of Travel Research, 36(1), 35–43.

Cossens, J. (1989). Positioning a tourist destination: Queenstown – a branded destination? Unpublished Ph.D thesis. New Zealand: University of Otago.

Crompton, J.L. & McKay, S.L. (1997). Motives of visitors attending festival events. Annals of Tourism Research, 24(2): 425–439.

Cronin, J. J. & Taylor, S. A. (1992). Measuring service quality: a reexamination and extension. Journal of Marketing, 56, 55–68.

Day, E. & Crask, M.R. (2000). Value assessment: the antecedent of customer satisfaction. Journal of Consumer Satisfaction, Dissatisfaction and Complaining Behaviour, 13: 42–50.

De Rojas, C. & Camarero, C. (2008). Visitors' experience, mood and satisfaction in a heritage context: evidence from an interpretation center. Tourism Management, 29, 525–537.

Dimitriades, Z.S. (2006). Customer satisfaction, loyalty and commitment in service organizations. Management Research News, 29(12): 782–800.

Echtner, & Brent Ritchie, J.R. (2003). The meaning and measurement of destination image. The journal of tourism studies, vol. 14, no. 1.

Ekinci, Y. & Chen, J.S. (2002). Segmenting overseas British holidaymakers by personal values. Journal of Hospitality & Leisure Marketing, Vol. 9 No. 3/4 pp. 5-15.

Embacher, J. & Buttle, F. (1989). A repertory grid analysis of austria's image as a summer vacation destination. Journal of Travel Research, 28(3): 3–23.

Fodness, D. (1994). Measuring tourist motivation. Annals of Tourism Research, 21(3): 555-581.

Formica, S. & Uysal, M. (1996). A market segmentation of festival visitors: Umbria jazz festival in Italy. Festival Management & Event Tourism, 3(4): 175–182.

Formica, S. & Murrmann, S. (1998). The effects of group membership and motivation on attendance: An international festival case. Tourism Analysis, 3(3–4): 197–207.

Fornell, C. (1992). A national customer satisfaction barometer: the Swedish experience. Journal of Marketing, 55: 1–21.

Fornell, C. & Larcker, D. F. (1981), "Evaluating Structural Equation Models with Unobservable Variables and Measurement Error". Journal of Marketing Research, 18(2): 39-50.

Fridgen, J. D. (1996). Dimensions of tourism. Educational Institute. MI: AHMA.

Fuchs, M. & Weiermair, K. (2003). New perspectives of satisfaction research in tourism destinations. Tourism Review, 58(3): 6–14.

Gartner, W. (1993). Image formation process. In communication and channel systems in Tourism Marketing Uysal, M. & Fesenmaier, D. eds., pp. 191–215. New York: Haworth Press.

Gallarza, M. & Saura, I. (2006). Value dimensions, perceived value, satisfaction and loyalty: an investigation of university students' travel behaviour. Tourism Management, 27: 437–452.

Gratton & Taylor, (1987). Leisure and shopping. The domesday experience. Journal Leisure Management,Vol. 7 No. 3 pp. 29-30.

Gronroos, C. (1984). A service quality model and its marketing implications. European Journal of Marketing, 18: 36–44.

Guenzi, P. & Pelloni, O. (2004). The impact of interpersonal relationships on customer satisfaction and loyalty to the service provider. International Journal of Service Industry Management, 15(4), 365–384.

Gursoy, D., McCleary, K. W. & Lepsito, L. R. (2007). "Propensity to Complain: Affects of Personality and Behavioral Factors." *Journal of Hospitality & Tourism Research*, 31 (3): 358-386.

Gursoy, D., McCleary, K. W. & Lepsito, L. R. (2003). "Segmenting Dissatisfied Restaurant Customers Based on Their Complaining Response Styles." *Journal of Food Service Business Research*, 6 (1): 25-44.

Gutiérrez Puebla, J. (1987). Spatial structures of networks flows: a graph theoretical approach. Transport Research B, 21B, 6, 489-502.

Hair, J.F., Anderson, R.E., Tatham, R.L. and William, C.B. (1995). Multivariate Data Analysis with Readings, Prentice-Hall, Englewood Cliffs, NJ.

Hair, J. F. J., Anderson, R. E., Tatham, R. L. & Black, W. C. (1998). Multivariate data analysis with readings. Englewood Cliffs, NJ: Prentice-Hall.

Hegarty, J.A. & O'Mahony, G.B. (2001). Gastronomy: A phenomenon of cultural expressionism and an aesthetic for living. International Journal of Hospitality Management, 20: 1, pp. 3–13.

Holbrook & Corfman, (1985). "Quality and Value in the Consumption Experience: Phaedrus Rides Again" in Perceived Quality: How Consumers View Stores and Merchandise, Lexington, MA: D. C. Heath and Company.

Homburg, C, & Giering, A. (2001). Personal characteristics as moderators of the relationship between customer satisfactiona and loyalty. Psychology and Marketing, 18: 43–66.

Hudman, L. E. (1986). The travelers perception of the role of food and eating in the tourist industry. In The Impact of Catering and Cuisine upon Tourism, Proceedings of 36th AIEST Congress, 31 August–6 September, Montreux: AIEST.

Husbands, W. (1989). Social Status and Perception of Tourism in Zambia. Annals of Tourism Research, 16: 237- 253.

Iso-Ahola, S. & Mannel, R. C. (1987). Psychological nature of leisure and tourism experience. Annals of Tourism Research, 14(3), 314-331.

Jacoby, J. & Chestnut, R.W. (1978). Brand Loyalty: Measurement and Management. New York: Wiley.

Jones, T.O. & Sasser, W.E. (1995). Why satisfied customers defect. Harvard Business Review, 73(6): 89–99.

Jones, A. & Jenkins, I. (2002). "A taste of wales—Blas Ar Gymru": Institutional malaise in promoting welsh food tourism products. Tourism and gastronomy, Routldge, London, pp. 113–115.

Jöreskog, K. & Sörbom, D. (1993). SPSS LISREL 8: User's reference guide. Chicago, IL: SPSS Inc.

Kahn, B.E. (1995). 'Consumer variety-seeking among goods and services'. Journal of Retailing and Consumer Services, Vol. 2 No. 3, pp. 139-48.

Kim Lien, 2010. Tourist motivation and activities: A case study of Nha Trang, Vietnam.

Kozak, M. & Rimmington, M. (2000). Tourist satisfaction with Mallorca, Spain, as an off-season holiday destination. Journal of Travel Research, 38(1), 260–269.

Law, C. (1993). Urban tourism: Attracting visitors to large cities. London: Mansell.

Law, C. (Ed.). (1996). Tourism in major cities, London: Thomson Business Press.

Lawson, F. & Baud-Bovy, M. (1977). Tourism and recreational development. London: Architectural Press.

Lew, A.A. (1987). A framework of tourist attraction research. Annals of Tourism Research 14, pp. 553–575.

Littrell, P. C., Billingsley, B. S. & Cross, L. H. (1994). The effects of principal support on special and general educators' stress, job satisfaction, school commitment, health, and intent to stay in teaching. Remedial and Special Education, 15(5): 297–310.

Lymberopolous, K., Chaniotakis, I. & Soureli, M. (2004). Opportunities for banks to cross-sell insurance products. Journal of Financial Services Marketing, 9(1): 34–48.

Macintosh, G. (2007). Customer orientation, relationship quality and relational benefits to the firm. Journal of Services Marketing, 21(3): 150– 159.

Mai, L.W. & Ness, M. R. (2006). A structural equation model of customer satisfaction and future purchase of mail-Order speciality food. International Journal of Business Science and Applied Management, 1(1), 1-13.

Mattila, A.S. (2001). The impact of relationship type on soncumer loyalty in a context of service failure. Journal of Service Research, 4(2): 91–101.

Mazanec, J. (Ed.). (1997). *International city tourism: Analysis and strategy.* London: Pinter.

Mazurski, D. (1989). Past Experience and Future Tourism Decisions. Annals of Tourism Research, 16:333–344.

McAlister, L. & Pessemier, E. (1982). Variety Seeking Behavior: An Interdisciplinary Review. Journal of Con- sumer Research, 9 (December), 311-322.

McColl-Kennedy, J., Daus, C. & Sparks, B. (2003). The role of gender in reactions to service failure and recovery. Journal of Service Research, 6(1): 66–82.

Mittal, V. & Kamakura, W.A. (2001). Satisfaction, repurchase intent and repurchase behavior: investigating the moderating effect of consumer characteristics. Journal of Marketing Research, 38(1): 131–142.

Mohsin, A. & Ryan, C. (2003). Backpackers in the northern territory of Australia. The International Journal of Tourism Research, 5(2), 113-121.

Mohr, K., Backman, K.F., Gahan, L.W. & Backman, S.J. (1993). An investigation of festival motivations and Moutinho, L. 1987. Consumer Behavior in Tourism. European Journal of Marketing 21(10): 5 - 44.

Ndubisi, N.O. (2006). Effect of gender on customer loyalty: a relationship marketing approach. Marketing Intelligence and Planning, 24(1): 48–61.

Nicholls, J.A.F., Gilbert, G.R. & Roslow, S. (1998). Parsimonious measurement of customer satisfaction with personal service and the service setting. Journal of Consumer Marketing, 15(3): 239–253.

Nickel, Ponpun, Albert, I. & Wertheimer (1979). "Factors Affecting Consumers' Images and Choices of Drugstores". Journal of Retailing, 55 (Summer), 71-79.

Niininen, O., Szivas, E. & Riley, M. (2004). Destination loyalty and repeat behaviour: an application of optimun stimulation measurement. International Journal of Tourism Research, 6: 439–447.

Nunnally, J. C. (1978). Psychometric theory. New York: McGraw-Hill

O'Brien, L. & Jones, C. (1995). Do rewards really create loyalty? Harvard Business Review, May/June: 75–82.

Oh, H. (1999). Service quality, customer satisfaction, and customer value: a holistic perspective. International Journal of Hospitality Management, 18, 67–82.

Oh, H. (2003). Price fairness and its asymetric effects on overall price, quality and value judgements: the case of an upscale hotel. Tourism Management, 24: 397–399.

Oliver, R. L. (1980). A cognitive model of the antecedents and consequences of satisfaction decisions. Journal of Marketing Research, 17, 460–469.

Oliver, R. (1993). Cognitive, affective, and attribute bases of the satisfaction response. Journal of Consumer Research, 20(December), 418–430.

Oliver, R.L. (1997). Satisfaction: A Behavioral Perspective on the Consumer. New York: McGraw-Hill.

Oliver, R.L. (1999).Whence consumer loyalty? Journal of Marketing 63: 33–44.

Olson, J. & Dover, P. (1979). Disconfirmation of consumer expectations through product trial. Journal of Applied Psychology (64), 179-189.

Oppermann, M. (2000). Tourism destination loyalty. Journal of Travel Research, 39(1): 78–84.

Page, S. (1994). *Urban Tourism*. London: Routledge.

Pallant, J.J. (2005). SPSS survival manual: a step by step guide to data analysis using SPSS for Windows (Version 12).

Parasuraman, A., Zeithaml, V. A. & Berry, L. (1985). A conceptual model of service quality and its implications for future research. Journal of Marketing, 49(4): 41–50.

Parasuraman, A., Zeithaml, V. A. & Berry, L. L. (1994). Reassessment of expectations as a comparison standard in measuring service quality: Implications for further research. Journal of Marketing, 58, 120–135.

Parroco, De cantis, S., Giambalvo, O. & Tomaselli, V. (2005). Turismo sommerso e qualità dei dati: identificazione e controllo degli errori di misurazione nell'indagine sulle isole Eolie. Isole Eolie: quanto turismo?!, Volume III, 41-54.

Peterson, R. (1994). A meta-analysis of Cronbach's coefficient alpha. Journal of Consumer Research, 21(2), 381–391.

Patterson, P.G. (2007). Demographic correlates of loyalty in a service context. Journal of Services Marketing, 21(2): 112–121.

Pedersen, P.E. & Nysveen, H. (2001). Shopbot banking: an exploratory study of customer loyalty effects. The International Journal of Bank Marketing, 19 (4/5) (2001), pp. 146–155.

Perdue, (2002). The influence of behavioral experience, existing images, and selected website characteristics. Journal of Travel & Tourism Marketing, Volume 11, Pages 21 – 38.

Peters, G. (1994). Benchmarking customer service. London: Financial Times-Pitman

Petrick, J.F., Morais, D.D. & Norma, W.C. (2001). An examination of the determinants of entertainment vacationers' intentions to revisit. Journal of Travel Research, 40: 41–48.

Petrick, J. F. & Backman, (2002). An examination of the construct of perceived value for the prediction of golf travelers' intentions to revisit. Journal of Travel Research, 41(1), 38–45.

Petrick, J. F. (2004). Are loyal visitors desired visitors? Tourism Management, 25(4): 463-470.

Pike, (2002). Destination image analysis - A review of 142 papers from 1973–2000. Tourism Management, 23(5): 541–549.

Pine, B. J., Peppers, D. & Rogers, M. (1995). Do you want to keep your customers forever? Harvard Business Review, March-April, 103-14.

Pitts & Woodside, (1986). Personal values and travel decisions. Journal of Travel Research, July 1986 25: 20-25.

Pizam, A., Neumann, Y. & Reichel, A. (1978). Dimensions of tourist satisfaction with a destination. Annals of Tourism Research, 5: 314-322.

Pritchard, M. & Howard, D.R. (1997). The loyal traveller: examining a typology of service patronage. Journal of Travel Research 35(4): 2–10.

Quan & Wang, (2004). Towards a structural model of the tourist experience: an illustration from food experiences in tourism. Tourism Management Volume 25, Issue 3, Pages 297-305.

Quintal, V.A. & Polczynski, A. (2011). Factors influencing tourists' revisit intentions. Asia Pacific. Journal of Marketing and Logistics, Vol. 22 No. 4, pp. 554-578.

Reichheld, F. & Teal, T. (1996). The loyalty effect: the hidden force behind growth, profits and lasting value. Boston, MA: Harvard Business School Press.

Reilly, M. D. (1990). Free elicitation of descriptive adjectives for tourism image assessment. Journal of Travel Research, 28(4):21–26.

Reisinger, Y. & Turner, L. W. (2003). Cross-cultural behaviour in tourism: Concepts and analysis. Oxford: Butterworth-Heinemann.

Riley, M., Niininen, O., Szivas, E.E. & Willis, T. (2001). The case for process approaches in loyalty research in tourism. Internationa Journal of Tourism Research, 3: 23–32.

Rispoli, M. & Tamma, M. (1995). Risposte strategiche alla complessità: le forme di offerta deiprodotti alberghieri. Giappichelli, Torino.

Rojas & Camarero (2006). International review on public and non profit marketing, Vol. 3, n° 1 pp. 49-65. Experience and satisfaction of visitors to museums and cultural exhibitions.

Russell, J. A. (1980). A circumplex model of affect. Journal of Personality and Social Psychology, 39, 1161–1178.

San Martin, H., Collado, J. & Rodriguez, I. (2008). El proceso global de satisfaccion bajo multiples estandares de comparacion: el papel moderador de la familiaridad, la involucracion y la interaccion cliente-servicio. Revista Espanola de Investigacion de Marketing ESIC, 12(1): 65–95.

Shoemaker, S. (1989). Segmentation of the senior pleasure travel market. Journal of Travel Research, 27(3):14-21.

Shoemaker, S. & Lewis, R. C. (1999). Customer loyalty: the future of hospitality marketing. International Journal of Hospitality Management, 18, 345–370.

Spreng, R.A. & Mackoy, R.D. (1996). An empirical examination of a model of perceived service quality and satisfaction. Journal of Retailing, 72(2): 201–214.

Stern, E. & Krakover, S. (1993). The formation of a composite urban image. Geographical Analysis, 25(2):130-146.

Tam, J. L. M. (2000). The effects of service quality, perceived value and customer satisfaction on behavioral intentions. Journal of Hospitality and Leisure Marketing, 6(4), 31–43.

Trong, H. & Ngoc, M. (2005). Research data analysis with SPSS.

Truong & Foster, (2006). Using HOLSAT to evaluate tourist satisfaction at destinations: The case of Australian holidaymakers in Vietnam. Tourism Management, 27: 842–855.

Truong & King, (2009). An Evaluation of Satisfaction Levels among Chinese Tourists in Vietnam. International Journal Of Tourism Research Int. J. Tourism Res. 11, 521–535 Published online 15 March 2009 in Wiley InterScience.

Um, S. & Crompton, J. L. (1990). Attitude determinants in tourism destination choice. Annals of Tourism Research, 17:432-448.

Um, S., Chon, K. & Ro, Y. (2006). Antecedents of revisit intention. Annals of Tourism Research, 33 (4): 1141-1158.

Uysal, Backman & Potts, (1991). An examination of event tourism motivations and activities. New horizons in tourism and hospitality education, training and research: Conference proceedings, University of Calgary, Calgary, Canada (1991), pp. 203–218.

Uysal, M., Gahan, L. & Martin, B. (1993). An examination of event motivations: a case study. Festival Management & Event Tourism, 1(1): 5–10.

Uysal, M., Mclellan, R. & Syrakaya, E. (1996). Modelling vacation destination decisions: a behavioural approach. Recent Advances in Tourism Marketing Research, 57-75.

Valle, Silva, Mendes & Guerreiro, (2006). Tourist Satisfaction and Destination Loyalty intention: A Structural and Categorical Analysis. Journal of Business Science and Applied Management / Business-and-Management.com.

Valazques, Saura & Molina, (2011). Conceptualizing and measuring loyalty: Towards a conceptual model of tourist loyalty antecedents. Journal of Vacation Marketing, 17(1) 65–81.

Van Trijp, H.C.M., Hoyer, W.D. & Inman, J.J. (1996), 'Why switch? Product-category level explanations for true variety-seeking behavior'. Journal of Marketing Research, Vol. 33 No. 3, pp. 281-92.

Zabkar, V., Brenc, M. & Dmitrovic, T. (2010). Modelling perceived quality, visitor satisfaction and behavioural intentions at the destination level. Tourism Management, 31, 537-546.

Walmsley, D. J. & Jenkins, J. M. (1993). Appraisive images of tourist areas: Application of personal construct. Australian Geographer, 24(2), 1–13.

Wnag & Hsu, (2010). The relationships of destination image, satisfaction, and behavioral intentions: An integrated model. Journal of Travel & Tourism Marketing, 27: 829–843

Weber, K. (1996). The assessment of tourist satisfaction using the expectancy disconfirmation theory: a study of the German travel market in Australia. Pacific Tourism Review, 14: 35–45.

Williams, J. (1997). 'We never eat like this at home': food on holiday. In: Caplan, P., Editor, 1997. Food, health and identity, Routledge, London, pp. 151–171.

Wood, L.M. (2004). Dimensions of brand purchasing behavior: consumers in the 18–24 age group. Journal of Consumer Behavior, 4(1): 9–24.

Woodruff, R. B. (1997). Customer value: The next source for competitive edge. Journal of the Academy of Marketing Science, 25(2), 139–153.

Woodside, A., Frey, L. & Daly, R. (1989). Linking service quality, customer satisfaction and behavioral intention. Journal of Health Care Marketing, 9, 5–17.

Yates & Maanen, (2001). Information technology and organizational transformation. pp 305-306.

Yoon, Y. & Uysal, M. (2005). An examination of the effects of motivation and satisfaction on destination loyalty: a structural model. Tourism Management, 26(1): 45–56.

Yuksel, (2007). Shopping risk perceptions: effects on tourists' emotions, satisfaction and expressed loyalty intentions. Tourism Management, 28(3): 703–713.

Yu & Littrell, (2003). Product and Process Orientations to Tourism Shopping. Journal of Travel Research, 42: 140-150.

Zeithaml, V.A. (1988). Consumer perceptions of price, quality and value: a means-end model and synthesis of evidence. Journal of Marketing, 52(July): 2–22.

Zeithaml, V. A., Berry, L. L. & Parasuraman, A. (1996). The behavioral consequences of service quality. Journal of Marketing, 60(2), 31–46.

Zins, A.H. (2001). Relative attitudes and commitment in customer loyalty models. International Journal of Service Industry Management, 12(3): 269–294.

Websites:

http://www.cinet.vn/upLoadFile/HTML/main.htm

http://thuvienluanvan.com,

http://www.nhatrang-travel.com/index

http://vietwondertravel.com

http://www.wordiq.com/definition/Tourist_destination

APPENDIX
Survey questionnaire

Dear participants,

We are lecturers of Economics Faculty, Nha Trang University. We are conducting this thesis about "explaining tourist satisfaction and intention to visit/recommend to Nha Trang". The purpose of this study is to investigate tourists satisfaction, loyalty intention and willingness to recommend Nha Trang to others. In order to give some strategies for improving visitors satisfaction and loyalty intention of tourist visiting Nha Trang.

Thank you very much for your help!

Completing the questionnaire

Read each question carefully before you make your answer. Please find and select the alternative that most suits your feelings. You will not always find the answer alternative that best describes your attitudes and feelings. In this case, choose the alternative that is closest. The questionnaire contains questions where you set a cross in the square, and some questions require you to fill in a number.

We remind you that there are no right or wrong answers: we are interested in your feelings and opinions. It is very important that you answer all the questions! Your careful answer contribute to the success of this study.

Have you perfect days in Nha Trang, Viet Nam!

Hotel/Restaurant/Bar/Beach:..

Appendix 1. Some general information about the experience the visitor has with Nha Trang.

Below we would like you to describe your experiences with visiting Nha Trang? (One cross ☒ per line)

Appendix 1.1 How many times have you visited Nha Trang during the last 10 years?

1time	2 times	3 times	4 times	5 times	6 times	7 times	8 times	9 times	10 times	Over 10 times
❑	❑	❑	❑	❑	❑	❑	❑	❑	❑	❑

Appendix 1.2 How long time have you intended to stay this time?

1-2 days	3-6 days	7-10 days	11-14 days	15-20 days	3-5 weeks	6-9 weeks	10 weeks	More 10 weeks
❑	❑	❑	❑	❑	❑	❑	❑	❑

Appendix 1.3 What kind of accommodation are your mostly staying this year?

Hotel + stars   ❑   (.........stars)

Private (friends/ relatives)   ❑

Rent   ❑

Others (please write detail) ....

Appendix 2. Evaluation of different aspects or attributes with Nha Trang as a place to visit

Appendix 2.1 Destination image – facets and attributes

Below, we would like you to indicate how bad or good you evaluate the different destination attributes of Nha Trang, Viet Nam along a scale from 1 (very bad) to 7 (very good) (One cross ☒ per line).

Aspects or attributes	1	2	3	4	5	6	7	Other idea
Beauty of scenery	❑	❑	❑	❑	❑	❑	❑	
Attractiveness of city	❑	❑	❑	❑	❑	❑	❑	
Islands	❑	❑	❑	❑	❑	❑	❑	
Beaches	❑	❑	❑	❑	❑	❑	❑	
Cleanliness	❑	❑	❑	❑	❑	❑	❑	
Safety	❑	❑	❑	❑	❑	❑	❑	
Prices of accommodation	❑	❑	❑	❑	❑	❑	❑	
Communication skills of staffs	❑	❑	❑	❑	❑	❑	❑	
Quality of roads	❑	❑	❑	❑	❑	❑	❑	
Public transport	❑	❑	❑	❑	❑	❑	❑	
Hotels quality & service	❑	❑	❑	❑	❑	❑	❑	
Restaurants quality & service	❑	❑	❑	❑	❑	❑	❑	
Discotheques and clubs	❑	❑	❑	❑	❑	❑	❑	
Easy access to the area	❑	❑	❑	❑	❑	❑	❑	
Well communicated traffic flow	❑	❑	❑	❑	❑	❑	❑	
Hospitality of people	❑	❑	❑	❑	❑	❑	❑	
Friendliness of people	❑	❑	❑	❑	❑	❑	❑	
Cultural events/ festival	❑	❑	❑	❑	❑	❑	❑	
Sports activities	❑	❑	❑	❑	❑	❑	❑	
Fashionable	❑	❑	❑	❑	❑	❑	❑	
Night life	❑	❑	❑	❑	❑	❑	❑	
Shopping possibilities	❑	❑	❑	❑	❑	❑	❑	
Variety & uniqueness of foods	❑	❑	❑	❑	❑	❑	❑	
Quality of foods	❑	❑	❑	❑	❑	❑	❑	
Prices of foods	❑	❑	❑	❑	❑	❑	❑	

Appendix 2.2 Perceived quality

Please select and circle a cell that the most express the general attractiveness of Nha Trang city. (One cross ☒ per line)

	1	2	3	4	5	6	7	
Dull	❑	❑	❑	❑	❑	❑	❑	Exiting
Unattractive	❑	❑	❑	❑	❑	❑	❑	Attractive
Negative	❑	❑	❑	❑	❑	❑	❑	Positive
Bad	❑	❑	❑	❑	❑	❑	❑	Good
Distressing	❑	❑	❑	❑	❑	❑	❑	Relaxing

Appendix 3. Evaluation of satisfaction

Please indicate for each row which word best describes how you feel about your visit in Nha Trang on a scale from 1 (strongly disagree) to 7 (strongly agree) (One cross ☒ per line)

Appendix 3.1

Please indicate how much you agree with the following statements

	1	2	3	4	5	6	7
I really enjoyed the visit	❑	❑	❑	❑	❑	❑	❑
I am satisfied with my decision to visit Nha Trang	❑	❑	❑	❑	❑	❑	❑
I prefer this destination	❑	❑	❑	❑	❑	❑	❑
I have positive feelings regarding Nha Trang	❑	❑	❑	❑	❑	❑	❑
This experience is exactly what I need	❑	❑	❑	❑	❑	❑	❑
My choice to purchase this trip was a wise one	❑	❑	❑	❑	❑	❑	❑
This was a pleasant visit	❑	❑	❑	❑	❑	❑	❑
This visit was better than expected	❑	❑	❑	❑	❑	❑	❑

Appendix 4. Evaluation of Intentional loyalty

Please indicate for each row which word best describes how you think about your revisit in Nha Trang on a scale from 1 (strongly disagree) to 7 (strongly agree) (One cross ☒ per line)

Appendix 4.1 Recommendation

How much you agree with the following statements

	1	2	3	4	5	6	7
I will visit Nha Trang again in the future	❑	❑	❑	❑	❑	❑	❑
If I could have done it again, I would have chosen this destination	❑	❑	❑	❑	❑	❑	❑
I would recommend Nha Trang to others	❑	❑	❑	❑	❑	❑	❑
I speak positive about Nha Trang to others	❑	❑	❑	❑	❑	❑	❑

Appendix 4.2 Intention to revisit

For some, expectations, planning and desires mean the same thing. For others, there is a difference between the terms. Please indicate how likely is it that you will choose to visit Nha Trang within 3 years? (One cross ☒ per line)

	Very unlikely likely						Very
The next three years	1	2	3	4	5	6	7
I plan to visit …	❑	❑	❑	❑	❑	❑	❑
I want to visit …	❑	❑	❑	❑	❑	❑	❑
I expect to visit …	❑	❑	❑	❑	❑	❑	❑
I desire to visit …	❑	❑	❑	❑	❑	❑	❑

Appendix 5. Evaluation of variety seeking and demographic characteristics

Appendix 5.1 Variety seeking

Please indicate how much you agree with the following statements concerning your choice of travel destination (as a tourist) on a scale from 1 (strongly disagree) to 7 (strongly agree). (One cross ☒ per line)

	1	2	3	4	5	6	7
I like to visiting many different destinations	❑	❑	❑	❑	❑	❑	❑
I prefer to go to destinations I have not visit before	❑	❑	❑	❑	❑	❑	❑
I do not usually change destination I visit from time to time	❑	❑	❑	❑	❑	❑	❑
I would like to return to a destination I am familiar with	❑	❑	❑	❑	❑	❑	❑
I am curious about new destinations I am not familiar with	❑	❑	❑	❑	❑	❑	❑
I find myself visiting the same places time after time I am travelling	❑	❑	❑	❑	❑	❑	❑

Appendix 5.2 Demographic characteristics

Finally, we would like to ask you a little information about yourself.

1.What year were you born?(state only the last two numbers)

   19 ⬚

2.Gender (choose only one ☒)

   Male ❑   Female ❑

3.Where do you live?

   City/ province: Country:

4.What is your highest completed education? (One cross ☒)

   Lower education   ❑

   High school   ❑

   College degree   ❑

   University degree   ❑

   Post-graduate   ❏

5. What is the approximate total income per year in your household?

   Less $20,000   ❏
   $20,000 - $39,999   ❏
   $40,000 - $59,999   ❏
   $60,000 - $79,999   ❏
   $80,000 and over   ❏

Thank you for your participation and time to answer the question!

CPSIA information can be obtained at www.ICGtesting.com
Printed in the USA
LVOW101711141112

307323LV00008B/136/P

9 783659 107849